W0013008

Creative Writing

Richard Aczel

Ernst Klett Sprachen
Barcelona · Budapest · London · Ljubljana · Prag
Posen · Sofia · Stuttgart

Bibliographische Information der Deutschen Bibliothek.
Die Deutsche Bibliothek verzeichnet diese Publikation in der
Deutschen Nationalbibliographie; detaillierte bibliographische
Daten sind im Internet über http://dnb.ddb.de abrufbar

1. Auflage A1   5 4 3 2 1 | 2007 2006 2005 2004
© Ernst Klett Sprachen GmbH, Stuttgart 2004. Alle Rechte vorbehalten.
Internetadresse | http://www.klett-verlag.de
Bildnachweis | Albrecht Dürer, Rhinocerus
Picture-Alliance/akg-images/Erich Lessing

Redaktion | Margit Künzel
Umschlaggestaltung | Marion Köster
Satz | media office gmbh, Kornwestheim
Druck | Ludwig Auer GmbH, Donauwörth. Printed in Germany.
ISBN 3-12-939614-4

Contents

Preface

This book has grown out of the Creative Writing Seminar that I have been teaching for the last ten years at the University of Cologne. "Teaching" is perhaps not quite the right word. A course in Creative Writing – whether a seminar or a book like this – doesn't so much seek to teach as to enable. This book assumes that you, the reader, have things you want to say, and it suggests some tools and techniques that will, I hope, enable you to say them better. Some of these tools and techniques have to do with getting more closely in touch with what it is you want to say; others have to do with the craft of saying them in such a way that others will want to hear them.

I am particularly grateful to Ansgar Nünning, the editor of the Klett "UNI WIS-SEN, Anglistik-Amerikanistik" series, for giving me the opportunity to bring together in the form of a book some of the things I have learnt from working over the years with groups of inspiringly dedicated student-writers in Cologne. I should also like to thank Frank Kearful, Selwyn Jackson, Tim Jones, and Ulla Iken for their valuable comments on the manuscript.

Richard Aczel
September, 2004

Introduction: Dürer's Rhinoceros

Focus

This book is above all for people who want to write fiction or poetry of any shape or kind. It offers a practical, step-by-step guide to tapping creative resources, generating ideas, and turning these ideas into convincing, well-crafted and readable pieces of writing.

The book is written in the firm belief that good writing is, on the whole, less the product of divine inspiration or inborn genius, than of hard work and sensible, regular practice. Genius and inspiration are great if and when you have them, but even the very best writers can't count on having them twenty-four hours a day. Writers are no different from other artists – painters, composers, ballet dancers, opera singers, musicians. A lot of hard slog goes into every fraction of apparently effortless achievement. They have to practise daily and there are things they have to work at a thousand times before they get them right. Those who become really good are those who don't give up when the going gets tough.

Desire

This is where personality and temperament come in. You can learn to play your triplets on the piano that little bit faster, to sing a semitone higher, to get that leg straighter, that brush-stroke finer, but what no one can teach you is to want to do these things enough to stay with them when all seems pointless or lost. That desire, that will, has to come from within and it has to be very strong indeed.

Imagination

In 1515, ALBRECHT DÜRER made a drawing and a woodcut of a rhinoceros. The remarkable thing was that he had never actually seen a rhinoceros in his life. Earlier that year, an Indian rhinoceros had been shipped to Lisbon as a gift to the King of Portugal. It was later sent on to Rome as a gift to POPE LEO X, but the boat that carried it sank *en route* and the animal was lost. Although DÜRER covered his creature with plates and scales, a saw-like back and an extra horn, his drawing was reproduced in natural history books up until the nineteenth century. DÜRER's rhinoceros is both ferocious and fastidious, wild and well-proportioned. It is a work of the imagination produced with such enormous technical skill that the image, once seen, is unforgettable.

Well-trained Rhinos

Creative Writing is all about the yoking of imagination to technique. This book can't give you an imagination that you don't possess, but it can tickle the one you have and help it produce ideas it didn't even know it had. The book may not be able to make you a DÜRER of the written word, but it can help you develop techniques to put your ideas into words that others will want to read.

"My poems," writes ANDREW MOTION, the British Poet Laureate, *"are the product of a relationship between a side of my mind which is conscious, alert, educated and manipulative, and a side which is as murky as a primaeval swamp. I can't predict when this relationship will flower."* As a teacher of Creative Writing, as well as a writer, ANDREW MOTION would surely agree that, while this flowering remains fundamentally precarious and unpredictable, there are things one can do to give it the best possible chance of occurring. This book looks at both the murky and the manipulative sides of the writer's work, and at how the two sides can be trained to complement each other.

Poetry and Prose

This is a book for writers of both fiction and poetry. I'd be happy if the poets also did all the fiction exercises and the story-tellers did the poetry ones. Poets and prose writers have a lot to learn from one another. Good prose is no less crafted than good poetry and should be able to stand up to the same critical scrutiny. All the chapters and sections on generating ideas and kick-starting the imagination are equally relevant to writers of poetry and prose. So please don't just jump to the poetry chapters if you're a poet and to the fiction chapters if you want to write prose.

Contents

Chapter 1 on "Getting Started" is definitely for scribblers of all species. It looks at ways of thinking like a writer, of training the senses, and of generating ideas.

Chapter 2 ("Telling Stories: Setting Out") looks at where our stories come from, and at how we can draw on our own experience in our imaginative writing. Although the emphasis is on writing short fiction, the sections on "Finding our Stories" and "Story Resources" are equally relevant to the writing of poetry.

Chapter 3 ("Telling Stories: The Nuts and Bolts") gets down to the nitty-gritty of story-telling. It focuses on four fundamental build-ing-blocks of narrative fiction – character, setting, voice and per-spective – and also looks at ways of beginning and ending stories.

In **Chapter 4** ("Telling a Story Again) we start putting some of the ideas of the previous chapters into practice. We create one basic story outline, then re-write the story in several different ways, experimenting with different styles, sequences, narrators and points of view.

Chapter 5 ("Writing Poems: Breaking Lines") asks some basic questions about writing poetry. What are poems, and why do we write and read them? It looks at these questions from the point of view of the poet, and in answering them already begins to explore ways of finding our own poems and making them of interest to the ears and eyes of others.

Chapter 6 ("Writing Poems: Sound and Sense") offers a hands-on approach to poetic form. It is a chapter about the craft of writing for the ear. It focuses on the essential elements that constitute the sound-world of our poems, such as rhythm, metre, and rhyme.

In **Chapter 7** ("Writing Poems: Form and Finish") we move on to working with given poetic forms such as the haiku, the sonnet, and the sestina. We also talk about revising our poems and extending them into groups and cycles.

Chapter 8 ("Creative Writing and the University") is a bit more theoretical. On the basis of the work done in the previous seven chapters, it offers some reflections about the role and value of Creative Writing as a university discipline.

Finally, there is a brief Appendix on "Creative Writing Workshops".

Exercises

All the chapters are exercise-based. (There are even two exercises in the more theory-oriented Chapter 8.) Many of the exercises are marked separately with the margin-word "Exercise". Many others are built into the main body of other paragraphs. Most of the exercises are short and won't take more than ten or twenty minutes of your time. Some are longer, involving processes of re-writing or observation spreading across several days. Some are no more than questions for you to take away and think about. Most of the exercises are worth doing more than once. Go back to ones you've already done after a couple of weeks and try them again.

Work

This is a work-book, and writing is hard work. The more you put in, the more you get out. All writing is *poiesis*: "making" – and the more things you make, the better maker you become.

Joy

Writing is also a great joy. There are few things in life as exciting as seeing stories and characters and rhythms and rhinoceroses emerge from what Shakespeare called "aery nothing". Once you've got the bug of jotting things down in notebooks and seeing them grow in shapes and forms that you'd never expected, you'll never be able to kick the habit. So, work hard, have fun, and above all *surprise yourself.*

CHAPTER Getting Started

1 Thinking Like a Writer

There are as many different types of writer as there are different types of writing. Some writers are great talkers, others only come alive verbally through the written word. Some plan every stage of their work from beginning to end, others might start out with a single image, turn of phrase or inflection of voice. Some work best at regular hours in the day, others write in fits and starts. Most generalizations about writers and their habits and methods are true of some writers and untrue of others. So the phrase "thinking like a writer" has to be taken fairly loosely. I am sure there are plenty of first-rate writers who would not recognize themselves in the picture of "the writer" offered by even the most helpful of Creative Writing handbooks. And it is very important that you too should feel perfectly free to say to yourself "that just isn't me", or "that's not how I think or work", when faced with some of the statements and exercises offered by this book.

At the same time, however, there are certain habits of mind and certain basic truths that most people concerned with the imaginative use of the written word would hold to be fairly essential. Most writers would agree that writing is a bit like playing a musical instrument: you have to practise regularly, and careful, focused practice will enable you to get better.

Writers

The French poet MALLARMÉ once said: the purpose of all the world is to be turned into a book. Every aspect of human experience, however ordinary or everyday, is of interest to the writer. Any action, event, or observation can very easily find its way into a piece of writing that you happen to be doing. Imagine you are writing a short story. There may come a moment when you will have to get a character on or off a bus or bicycle. You may have to describe the creaking of a door or the breaking of a glass. Or your character may be simply bending down to tie his or her shoes. If you have never seen or heard any of these things, you will find it hard to describe them. If, on the other hand, you habitually take mental note of such things when you see or hear them, you will have a range of pictures and sounds at your fingertips. Writers are forever on the lookout. They are compulsive observers. Perhaps the best advice ever offered by one great writer to other would-be writers was that given by the American novelist, HENRY JAMES, in his "The Art of Fiction" (1884): "Try to be one of the people on whom nothing is lost". (JAMES 1963: 86)

On the Lookout

Interest

The knowledge that everything can be of use transforms the world for you as a writer. Even at the most boring party, you can get lucky and spot a gesture or overhear a phrase that fits perfectly into the piece of writing you are currently working on, or even a piece you hadn't yet thought of. This doesn't mean that writers are never bored at parties. Sometimes they are happy just to be discussing the weather, or drowning their sorrows in a glass of wine. But they rarely switch off altogether. Learning to write has as much to do with developing your powers of observation as with developing your skills with words.

Notebooks

Unless you have a photographic memory, observations aren't much good to you if you don't write them down. A notebook – i. e. a book in which to scribble observations with a pen, and not a laptop computer! – is an absolute essential for a writer. The very first thing to do, if you are serious about starting to write, is to go and get yourself a good notebook. It needs to be something solid, from which the pages don't fall out. You may want to look things up months or even years after you jotted them down. The size and shape is up to you. Some writers like something small they can carry in a pocket, others like more room to spread out. Some like lined pages and others prefer blank ones so that they can draw pictures to remind them of what they've seen. The important thing is to make sure you write in your notebook every day and that you date your entries. There's nothing more frustrating than remembering roughly when you jotted something down but not being able to find it in your notebook.

Reading

Writers are avid readers. They are naturally curious about what other writers have to say and how they say it. Reading is as much a part of the everyday activity of a writer as looking and listening and note-taking. The idea that you should read less to keep yourself free of influences is completely spurious. All writers learn from the books they read, and would never have written the way they do if they hadn't. For a writer, it is crucial to read widely. This means knowing the great works of the language, but also having a strong sense of what is being written now. No one wants to read books that sound like the last fifty years have not happened. You have to hear the voice of your own time, even if you decide that isn't how you want to sound.

Reading as a Writer

Writers not only read widely, they also read differently. Most of us read for information, entertainment, and the pure pleasure of a good plot or an apt expression. Writers are also interested in the mechanics of the texts they read. How has the author managed to achieve this or that effect, and what can I learn from his or her strengths and weaknesses? Reading is one of the essential ways of learning the tricks of the trade. Writers are very critical, but also very appreciative readers. They know how hard the job of writing is.

Writers are inevitably people who are fascinated by language in all shapes and sizes. They are perpetually on the lookout for ways of extending their verbal means of expressing ideas and responding to the world. This involves an openness to different types of language. Don't only read things you like, or things you already know you're interested in. Make a conscious effort to read things outside the range of your present interests and tastes. Pick up local newspapers, cookery books, advertizing brochures, instruction manuals, fashion magazines, anthologies of parliamentary speeches, comic books, popular science journals, seventeenth century sermons. Try to read at least one piece of writing a day that doesn't fit into your own verbal world.

Above all, write every day. Practice is the real key to improvement as a writer. Here again it is important to scribble regularly in notebooks, or to keep a diary. The writer NICOLE WARD-JOUVE has compared her diaries to writerly gymnastics.

Practice

It's like being a dancer or a musician. Unless you practise, you don't develop the muscles, or the suppleness, or the nimbleness of fingers. (BELL/MAGRS 2001: 13)

Get in the habit of writing daily, even if you feel you have nothing important to say. Regular writing will free you up. Knowing that you don't always have to be forging a memorable line of poetry or a sentence of judicious prose can take a good deal of weight off your shoulders. A lot of eminently forgettable writing usually goes into the production of something really good, and knowing what to scrap and being able to scrap it are two of the most important skills a writer has to learn.

Also, you never know what is going to come out of an apparently routine exercise. Sometimes, it will simply be a question of oiling the machinery or training the muscles. Occasionally, a seemingly mechanical exercise can put you in touch with an idea you didn't know you had.

2 Training the Senses

A piece of writing creates a world. Whether this world is meant to resemble our own or to be entirely fictional, it must still be convincing as a world. It is above all the observation of detail that makes a created world convincing. Listen to the poet PHILIP LARKIN going into a church:

Observation

Once I am sure there's nothing going on
I step inside, letting the door thud shut.
Another church: matting, seats, and stone,
And little books; sprawlings of flowers, cut
For Sunday, brownish now; some brass and stuff
Up at the holy end; the small neat organ;
And a tense, musty, unignorable silence,
Brewed God knows how long. Hatless, I take off
My cycle-clips in awkward reverence.
("Church Going")

The observations are so precise, and the detail so characteristic of the observer's view of the observed, that even not knowing the right names for things becomes an accuracy of observation.

Being in Touch

It is crucial to get in touch with the world of images, sounds, smells, and tastes around you. The more fully you perceive your world, the more convincingly you will be able to put it into words.

Of all our senses, sight and hearing are perhaps the most actively used in our everyday lives. Every day, we see our way through a multitude of spaces and situations while listening, above all, to the words and voices of others. The other senses tend to be relatively neglected. This imbalance is often reflected when we try to suggest sensuous experience in our writing. When we read, we are made to see things and to hear, first and foremost, what people say. The best writing, however, makes full and evocative use of the other senses. It is equally possible to suggest what an article of clothing is like through describing how it feels on one's skin as through describing the way it looks. One can say a great deal about one person's reaction to another by describing the smell of their skin or clothes. One can get very close to evoking the feel of the air – by the sea, in a forest, or in a stuffy library – by describing the taste it leaves on one's tongue.

Exercise

1. Go for a walk in the park. Stand still under a tree and listen. What noises can you hear? Listen carefully, until you can hear all the sounds around you, from the chatter of birds to the rush of distant traffic. Try to separate all the sounds in your head. Then write them down, one by one, describing them as carefully as you can. For example, don't just write birdsong; write a few words that accurately describe the noises made by different birds. Sometimes the sounds they make are more like sporadic machine-gunfire than singing.

2. Do the same thing with the senses of smell and touch. Pick things up and smell them. Hold them to your cheek and lips; trace their contours with the tips of your fingers. Write down lists of words and expressions that describe exactly what you perceive. Try this with

different metals, like brass, copper, tin, and steel; and with different types of wood: ebony, walnut, mahogany, oak, teak, chestnut, pine. In addition to learning the differences between their textures, find out their different uses. Enjoy the names, and the differences they stand for, and make use of them in your writing.

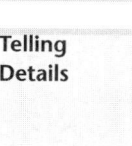

Telling Details

Detail is one of the keys to good writing, whether poetry or prose. But not all details are helpful; or rather, we are not interested in detail for its own sake. We need to choose those details that tell us something important about the world or situation being evoked. We'll be saying more about this in Chapter 3.

Seeing Differently

Good writing tends to make us look at the world differently. It can do this only because the writer has succeeded in seeing the world differently and has managed to put his or her individual vision across. One way of looking at our world differently is to look at it with someone else's eyes. Imagine someone from a different city, country, culture, continent, or even planet, seeing your street for the first time. What kind of things would they notice? What things would they see that you tend to overlook? Have a look at CRAIG RAINE's poem "A Martian sends a postcard home".

Exercise

Go and sit in your favourite café. Imagine you are there for the first time and come from a world where they don't have cafés. How do you make sense of what is going on? Why do people come here when, presumably, they all have coffee and tea at home?

We also see differently when we are in extreme situations. The park at the bottom of the street can look very different when you have just fallen in love, or when you feel wretchedly alone, or are completely preoccupied with the memory of something that took place there many years ago.

Version 1.

Sit in your favourite café again. This time, imagine that you have a secret to hide. What is your secret and why is it so terrible? Look at the people around you. Do any of them look back? Do they look at you suspiciously? Do they know something? And the ones who are ignoring you – are they doing it on purpose, when in fact they know full well that you have something to hide?

Version 2.

Imagine that you met someone in the café two years ago. It was a very important meeting. Perhaps you fell in love, or became unbelievably angry. Or perhaps something frightened you about that person, even though you couldn't say exactly what it was. You never met him or her again. Now you are back in the café for the first time since that meeting. Perhaps there is something in the waiter's or waitress's voice that reminds you of the person you met. Perhaps, under the table, you see the same shoes that he or she wore, and are terrified to look up. Describe the café, allowing everything to be coloured by what you felt then and what you are feeling now.

Discretion	Always remember to do your people-watching discreetly and respectfully. Writers are by nature nosy-parkers, but they need to develop very practical skills in observing without being noticed. One can gather all the necessary information without causing offence to other people or making them feel uncomfortable.

❸ Generating Ideas

Finding Your Ideas	We all have a rich store of images and incidents and stories just waiting to be turned into writing. This store is our memory. It is simply enormous. The trouble is, although we draw upon our memory all the time in our everyday lives, we only use a very small part of the store. There are rooms and rooms full of valuable material that we rarely get to see. First we have to learn how to gain access. This takes time and involves some hard and concerted effort. We have to develop the necessary tools to dredge up all the hidden treasures.
Automatic Writing	We shall be doing a lot of dredging exercises throughout this book. One exercise we'll be doing quite regularly is automatic writing. This involves writing rapidly and continuously on a particular subject without once pausing for thought or lifting your pen from the paper. Instead of stopping to think of what to say next, you go on writing anything, even complete and utter nonsense.
	The thing to remember is that even the most bizarre nonsense is coming from somewhere. It is coming from your unconscious store of images and ideas. It is precisely this unconscious store – this hidden iceberg of your memory – that we want to tap.
Exercise	Take a book and an egg-timer or stopwatch. Open the book at any page and choose at random five nouns (such as window, curtain, donkey, shoe, postbox). Turn over the egg-timer or set the stopwatch for one minute and start writing whatever comes into your head about the first noun. Write as quickly as you can. Don't stop to think and don't lift your pen from the page. If you're stuck, just go on writing anything: camel bells ringing in the monstrous owl garden strapped to marshmallow polar bears.
	Once the sand has run from the egg-timer, stop writing on the first noun, wherever you are, and start on the second. No break, no pause for thought, no getting to the end of an unfinished sentence.
	You can also do this exercise in pairs with a friend. Let the friend choose the words and watch the time. This means that you will have nothing to think about but keeping the pen moving across the page.
	Do these exercises straight into your notebook, or at least on pieces of paper you won't lose. Keep and store them. Your scribbles may

contain some very valuable material – the seeds or triggers for something bigger and more coherent. It may just be a single image or a turn of phrase that will lead you to an idea you didn't know you had. Do exercises like this every day. Go back regularly to what you have written. You will find a treasure trove, full of keys to your unconscious.

Keep Your Writing

The only way to start writing is to start writing.

Write

In a wise and quiet book on writing published seventy years ago, Dorothea Brande suggested that, when starting out, you should rise half an hour earlier than usual every day and, without speaking or reading the newspaper, begin to write whatever comes into your head. Just for half an hour. And every morning, religiously. Don't re-read what you did the previous morning. After a few days, you will begin to notice that your jottings reach a certain length without much effort. Try to push beyond this, just by a sentence or two, over the next few days. Later, you can even try to double your previous morning's output. Go back again, whenever you feel like it, to your earlier length, but periodically push just that little bit in order to do more.

Once you've got this going, start trying to reserve one other part of the day for writing. At first, just earmark half an hour. Don't use this time to work on a larger writing project. Keep it for a more open encounter with the page. Once you have set this time aside, don't let anything interrupt you. Brande calls this appointment you have made with the blank page a "debt of honour" (BRANDE 1996: 70).

I'd like to suggest that you put this book down now. Don't pick it up again for fourteen days. In that time, just keep writing, regularly and freely, as described. Get going with your early morning jottings. Try some automatic writing. Take your notebook to cafés, parks, other people's houses. Work on your senses, and on finding words for the things you see, hear, smell, taste, touch. Spend two weeks scribbling freely, forgetting entirely about that yet-to-be-written masterpiece. Then have a look at what you've done. Don't be disappointed: the aim wasn't to produce anything polished. Rather, be surprised – by the things that go round in your head, by the sound of your voice. What you have written will tell you something about where you are, as well as who you are, and where you are coming from as a writer. It will form a basis from which to start thinking about where you would like your writing to go. Remember, you can only build upon what's there. You've been stretching your muscles, exploring how the body of your writing naturally moves. When you sense that this body has limbered up and is beginning to be aware of its own movement, it's time to bring it back to this book for some more vigorous exercise.

Take Your Time

CHAPTER Telling Stories: Setting Out

1 First Thoughts

Focus

Together with Chapter 3, this chapter offers a basic toolkit for building stories. The aim is to do some elementary thinking about all the things that go into the making of a short story and to gain some practice and experience in trying them out.

The chapter focuses above all on generating ideas and thinking them into plots. Chapter 3 then goes into the nuts and bolts of story-telling, while Chapter 4 experiments with the techniques and methods we have been looking at in the context of a story that we'll be writing and rewriting in several different ways.

Note for Poets

Although the emphasis in this chapter is on writing stories, the sections on "Finding Our Stories" and "Story Resources" are just as relevant to the writing of poetry as to the writing of prose.

And Novelists

Almost everything we'll be saying and trying out in Chapters 2, 3, and 4 is equally relevant to the writing of a novel. Novels, too, live on plot, character, setting, perspective and voice. If you are writing a novel, I hope you will be able to come back to the exercises in these chapters again and again whenever you are stuck or simply in need of fresh ideas.

The Short Story

MALCOLM BRADBURY, in his Introduction to *The Penguin Book of Modern British Short Stories*, has called the short story "the most difficult of all prose forms of fiction". H.E. BATES, editor of *The Modern Short Story*, calls it "the most difficult and exacting of all prose forms". So why begin at the deep end? The answer is simply: because the short story is short. It gives us something that we can not only begin, but finish in a workable space of time. It offers a manageable testing ground for our ideas and methods and techniques.

Motivation

Why do you want to write a story? Do you already have a story to tell, or simply the desire to write one? Why should anyone want to read your story?

Perhaps a more helpful way of approaching the last question is to rephrase it: Why do you read stories? What are you looking for?

This is probably not a question you ask yourself very often, and it is not an easy question to answer. But it is a very important one, especially when it comes to writing stories yourself.

I suppose there are two basic reasons why we read stories. The first is to gain a glimpse of a world that we don't know; to be a fly on the wall witnessing events that we have never experienced, involving people we have never met. But we also like stories that tell us about our own world; about people – or types of people – and experiences that are familiar to us. Here, however, we are also looking for something new: a new perspective on a familiar situation, a new way of telling something that has perhaps been told a thousand times. This is rather like the eighteenth century poet ALEXANDER POPE'S definition of "true wit": "What oft was thought, but ne'er so well expressed."

Both of these basic expectations that we have when reading stories share one thing in common: the desire to be surprised. A story which merely confirms our view of the world in exactly the terms we normally see it may be gratifying or comforting, but it doesn't appeal to the genuine desire that motivates our reading. The pleasure we derive from being able to say "That's exactly what I think" to a friend at the bar who has been espousing political opinions we wholeheartedly share is very different from the pleasure of discovery afforded by a good piece of fiction.

That is why much of this chapter will be concerned with surprise. Throughout, I hope, we'll be surprising ourselves with things we didn't know we knew, and finding out how to share our surprises with others. This does not mean that we'll have to spend all our time trying to astonish or shock or stagger our readers. The surprises we are after are more modest affairs. But we do want to be able to catch our own interest and to hold that of the reader. This is what the "-prise" part of surprise literally means; it comes from Latin *praehendere*, to grasp or seize. We are rather like Coleridge's Ancient Mariner, detaining the busy wedding guests with a story they simply have to hear.

Surprise

The novelist GRAHAM SWIFT has described the essence of story-telling as "the relating of something strange". He compares the story-teller to the man in the pub who says things like "A funny thing happened to me…" or "You won't believe this, but…" Much of the surprise that fiction offers us derives from seeing things just a little differently. From bringing out the strange in the familiar and the familiar in the strange.

A Strange Thing

Finding Our Stories

You are a fascinating person, did anyone ever tell you? You've been through some pretty amazing things – not only in your dreams – and you've got thousands of stories to tell. Stories, what's more, that have never been told before. No? You don't think so?

The Primary Source

Well, it's true. However similar our everyday lives and our perceptions of the world we move around in, we all experience this world in a profoundly individual way. The great American short story writer Flannery O'Connor once said: "Anyone who has survived an average childhood has enough to write about for a dozen years."

The real challenge is to get in touch with the distinctiveness of your own experience: the true and authentic response to what you and only you have experienced and how you and only you have felt.

Often enough, of course, we don't perceive our world in a unique and individual way. We tend to see things through the eyes and expectations of others. We react as we've been taught to react, we respond as we imagine we are expected to respond. This is reflected in the language we use to describe our experiences. Often we simply use a kind of code: what we imagine to be the language of the "type" of people to whom we are speaking, or to whom we believe we belong. Something clearly gets lost in such a way of speaking. What gets lost is above all the distinctive quality of the experience in question, and the singularity of the way it has been felt.

Getting in Touch

Distinguishing between the way you respond to something and the ways in which you feel expected to respond is not easy. It takes honesty – and a certain amount of practice. Finding a language to formulate your distinctive experience of the world – a language that genuinely engages with what you have lived through, and a language that, for this very reason, is genuinely yours – takes a long time. In fact, it is a life's work for a writer. It has very little to do with striving to be "original". It has very little to do with trying to shake off every influence that has affected the way you perceive and speak and write. Influences are an essential part of your own individual experience of the world. You already are original without having to try. All you have to do is get in touch with your highly original self. All you have to do is get in the habit of seeing with your own eyes and speaking in your own voice.

Finding you own voice can be a long and arduous process. It is the same with finding your eyes. And ears, and nose, and sense of touch. Go back repeatedly to the exercises in Chapter 1 on "Training the Senses", to remind yourself of who you are, and how that "you" responds immediately to the world.

Imagination

Your own life and experience are obviously a major source for the stories you tell. Some of the greatest writing has come out of the most banal, everyday, personal experience. JAMES JOYCE'S *Ulysses* depicts, among other things, a very ordinary day in JOYCE'S Dublin, full of the people and places he knew best. It is of course many other things besides. It is, for example, an extraordinary work of the imagination.

One often hears the advice given to writers: "Write what you know". And very good advice it is. In part at least. But it's not the whole story. Here's GRAHAM SWIFT again:

My maxim would be: for God's sake write about what you don't know! For how else will you bring your imagination into play? How else will you discover or explore anything? (BOYLEN 1993: 24)

One of the reasons why we write and read is to imagine ourselves into worlds and experiences that are not our own. As the novelist HILARY MANTEL has put it: "write to find out – write to see what you know. You may surprise yourself." (BOYLEN 1993: 44)

Charity, they say, begins at home. So does writing. But it doesn't stay there forever. It ventures out into the wide world, hungry for adventure. Our own direct experience of life forms the foundations of most of what we write. Our imagination builds on these foundations. The house of our fiction, when it is finally built, is both self and other. It rises out of our own heartache, joy, belly-ache, despair, and stands before us as a stranger. Meeting this stranger, and watching him or her turn and go their own way in the world is one of the rare pleasures and rewards of writing.

Oneself as Another

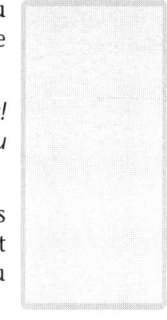

3 A Plot of One's Own

Starting small

Plot comes from plan *(complot)*. We also use it to describe a piece of earth or ground: a plot of land. This is, I think, a helpful way to begin thinking about plot in fiction. The plot is first and foremost your ground, a space where you go to get away from the chatter of everyday life, where you plant things and watch them grow.

Plot as Ground

The soil of this ground, this plot, is your language. I don't mean just the language you speak, a national language, like English, German or French. I mean your own language, your personal idiom, rooted in the vocabulary of memory, and in the most primal and personal verbal noises you make in your encounter with the world.

Admittedly, this might sound a long way from "plot" in the traditional literary sense: the grand plan for your novel, stretching in flowcharts and arrow diagrams from wall to wall of your study. This kind of planning is absolutely essential, and we'll come to it in due course. For the moment, however, I want to stay on the ground. I want you to think of plot not so much as the outline of a story as the soil stories spring from.

Finding your Ground	In Chapter 2, we talked about the importance of writing every day – anything, anywhere. The things you write when you are not writing "to order", as it were – even when you are not working on a clearly conceived story – should tell you a lot about the things that really concern you. Are there ideas that emerge time and again? Are there rhythms, patterns, images and individual words that seem to keep coming back? These tentative clusters of concerns, these hints of an emerging voice are the first markings of your ground, the first square inches of your plot. The more you go on writing, the wider and deeper that ground will become. But there will be something about the texture, the consistency, the colour and the smell of the soil that will always be fundamentally yours.
Seeds	The next step, of course, is to make that soil bear fruit. And here, to carry the metaphor one last stage further, you need seeds. HENRY JAMES used the term "germs": the embryo within the seed, that elementary micro-organism which is capable of turning into something else. For JAMES, "germs" often took the form of a snippet of story he'd heard over dinner. His notebooks are a wonderful testament to what happened to these fragments when they entered the fertile ground of his imagination. They make fascinating and inspiring reading for any writer. Just look at these excerpts from JAMES'S notebooking, over a period of four years, the germ of his novel *What Maisie Knew*:
November 12th, 1892	*Two days ago, at dinner at James Bryce's, Mrs. Ashton, Mrs. Bryce's sister, mentioned to me a situation that she had known of, of which it struck me immediately that something might be made in a tale. A child ... was divided by its parents in consequence of their divorce. The court ... decreed that* [the child] *was to spend its time equally with each* [parent] *– that is alternately. ... Suppose the real parents die, etc. – then the new parents marry each other in order to take care of it, etc. The basis of almost any story, any development would be that the child should prefer the new husband and wife to the old...*
December 22nd, 1895	*I have put my pen to the little subject of the child, the little girl whose parents are divorced, and then each marry again, leaving her divided between the 2nd husband of the one and the 2nd wife of the other. But the thing, before I go further, requires some more ciphering out, more extraction of the subject, of the drama – if such there really be in it. Voyons un peu* ["Let's see a little"] *– what little drama does reside in it? – I catch it, I catch it: I seize the tail of the little latent action qu'il recèle* ["that it conceals"]. *I made a mistake above, in thinking – in speaking – of the divorced parents as "dying": they live – the very essence of the subject is in that. Make that my point of view, my line, the consciousness, the dim, sweet, sacred, wondering, clinging perception of the*

CHAPTER **2** Telling Stories: Setting Out

child, and one gets something like this. The parents become indifferent to her as soon as they have her to quarrel about; then each marry again.

[On Sir Claude, the second "father" of Maisie, the child]... *He must be very nice very charming to Maisie, but he must get a little tired of her. As the whole thing is an action, so the little chapter is its little piece of the action; and to what point must the latter be brought by it? Voyons, voyons. Don't I see the whole thing reflected in the talk, the confidences, the intercourse of Mrs. Wix* [Maisie's Governess]*?*

October
26th, 1896

"*Voyons, voyons*" – let's see, let's see; JAMES's Notebooks are full of this phrase. This is how he works, thinking aloud, using his note-books to explore ideas. Just listen to the excitement as he begins to see – "I catch it, I catch it" – the special line that he needs to take! The notes are a little potboiler in themselves.

Story resources

HENRY JAMES, as we have seen, often took the skeleton of a story from an anecdote overheard at dinner. But we don't have to wait for an entertaining dinner guest in order to come up with anecdotes of our own.

Memory

Our memories are full of stories, even if we don't have immediate access to them all the time. Because the memory is such an important treasure house for the writer, gaining easy access to it is one of the most important things s/he can learn.

Gaining access to the memory is a bit like looking for something on the Internet. In order to find what you are after, you don't type in everything there is to know about the topic. If you could, you wouldn't need to do an Internet search in the first place. What you do is type in a keyword.

Triggers

It's the same with our memories. We can't go searching for them whole. We have to find appropriate triggers to bring them up on our mental screens. As with the Internet search, we have to be patient. Sometimes the first keyword doesn't bring us any relevant results. So we try another one, then another. The more we use search machines, the better we become at knowing in advance the best type of keyword to try.

You will need to experiment a bit to get to know which triggers work best to access all the stories echoing around in your memory, waiting to be told. Here are some triggers you can try.

Go back in your mind to the house you lived in as a child. Try to picture a particular chair in the living room, the kitchen, or in your bedroom. Shut your eyes and begin to see this chair very

Furniture

clearly. What did it look like? How did it feel on your body? Did it have a particular smell? Did it creak when you sat down or got up, was there a faint echo of a broken spring? Write down a very exact description.

Now picture someone sitting in it. It could be you as a child, or perhaps it wasn't a chair you sat in. Who sat in it? Was it your grandmother's chair? Your father's? Let a scene emerge in which you or somebody else is sitting in that chair. What else is going on? Does a memory begin to take shape? Has your grandmother fallen asleep over her knitting and are you and your brother whizzing paper aeroplanes over her head? Has someone just come in with important news? Does someone get up from the chair, or sink back into it?

Comment

I remember being in a Chinese restaurant with the Hungarian novelist PÉTER NÁDAS. There was a variety of sauces on the table and he was opening them all and smelling them. Among them was a bottle of H.P. sauce. "Ah," he said when he had taken a whiff, "this is exactly the smell of my grandmother's brown corduroy settee. The cushions were worn and shiny from all the bums that had sat on them. And the shiny bits smelt just like this sauce."

Did the chair trigger work for you? If not, try another piece of furniture. For example, a bed. Here's a list of beds you might try.

– Your first bed.
– Your parents' bed.
– A hospital bed.
– The first bed you slept in with someone else.
– The smell of your present bed, first thing in the morning.

Then try tables and cupboards, doors and windows.

Clothes

Clothes are another fruitful trigger. They are very intimately connected with our bodies and the way we feel about ourselves. Think of a dress or suit you had to wear for some fancy occasion as a child. Again, concentrate very hard and give yourself plenty of time to see it, feel it, smell it, very clearly. How do you feel in this getup? Why are you wearing it, what is going on?

Do the same for shoes and boots. Remember a pair you used to wear. Put them on again in your mind. Start walking. Where are they taking you?

Photographs

Photographs are great story-tellers. Or rather, they tell one bit of the story and leave the rest to the imagination. This is just the kind of trigger you need.

Look at some photographs from your childhood. What is going on in the picture? Try to fill in what happened before and what happened next. How did you feel? What were you thinking? If anyone seems to be talking in the photo, what are they saying?

 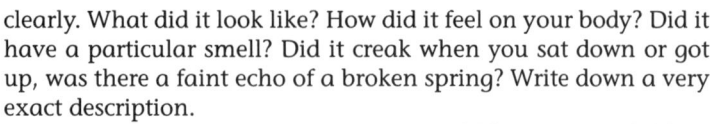

I have a photograph of my Uncle Mac raising his fist at the camera and showing off his forearm. I know what he was saying; it's what he always said: "Smell beef!" I never knew what this meant as a child, but the smell of roast beef always came to mind whenever he said it. Now I know – or think I do – that he was talking about his strength. This was funny, because by then he was a rather feeble old man. I can imagine a story beginning: "'Smell beef!' said Uncle Mac, shaking his fist." It would, I think, be a story about a child's view of an old man, and the old man's memories of a younger self that child never knew.

Look at photographs of members of your family you never knew. Try to imagine their lives. Talk to people who knew them. What you will get are fragments. Try to start filling in the gaps with your imagination. This is what story-telling is all about.

Fragments

All sorts of fragments make good triggers – not just for the memory, but for the imagination. A piece of broken china can suggest a whole cup, a lost cup, a lost tea-set. Trying to rebuild the pieces around it can lead you to the imagination of a whole world of stories. What kind of cup does the fragment suggest? What kind of family might have used it? How did it get broken? Try to reconstruct, as a labour of love, the world to which the fragment belonged.

Look out for fragments of all kinds. They might be snippets of overheard conversation that suggest a story whose gaps need filling in, imagining. Or they might be broken or displaced things, like the shard of china. Think of good places near you where you are likely to find fragments. Flea markets are always good. So are rivers. Whenever you next find yourself on the banks of a river, try this:

River-Rubbish

Pick your way among the rubbish thrown up by a river. Look out for potentially interesting objects. They don't have to be extraordinary things. A shoe will do, or a glove, or a bicycle pump. Who do you imagine these things belonged to? How did they get them, when and where did they wear them, what did they do with them? How did they end up in the river?

Look out for things that might have had more than one owner. Try to write the histories of these objects.

Comment

You may find that what you've written is a complete and pleasing short story. But don't worry if this is not the case. All you are really looking for here is one flash of an idea. In imaginatively putting together the stories of the things you have found, there may just be that one connection that really takes your fancy. The shoe may have belonged to the one-legged barman who always threw one of a pair away. Once he hobbled out of the bar to catch a woman who'd left her handbag on the counter. Instead, as he

turned the corner, he bumped into the strait-laced librarian he'd had his eye on for weeks. It's the expression on the librarian's face when she stands back and wonders what a one-legged barman is doing with a handbag dangling from his arm that interests you. The whole thing has nothing to do with shoes anymore.

The Past

Our pasts are full of fragments that can form the germs of stories. It may just be a turn of phrase used by a relative, or it may be the vague memory of a building or plot of land that is no longer there. As a child, I used to play in a field behind our house. It had once been the very extensive garden of a wealthy neighbour. For most of my childhood, the house was derelict and the field, as we called it, was gradually being turned into a building site. At one end was a half-burnt-down wooden hut we used to call the pavilion. It was actually a pavilion in the days when the house still flourished and there were tennis courts beside it. But by then it was simply a fire-gutted, ramshackle shed where we would take shelter from the rain. What I remember most strongly was the drumming of the rain on the unceilinged roof. Years later, I was in a tiny church in East Sussex when it started to rain and I heard exactly the same drumming and felt exactly as if I were back in the pavilion in the field. But I can't go back there any more, except in my thoughts, because it's all blocks of flats now. I'm sure there's a story somewhere in all this.

Seeing Yourself

Here is short poem by THOMAS HARDY (1840–1928) called "The Self Unseeing". It's about not being fully aware of things as they happen and looking back at them with a pang when they're past. See if you can create a similar scene of your own. You may be able to use it as the basis for a story.

Here is the ancient floor,
Footworn and hollowed and thin,
Here was the former door
Where the dead feet walked in.

She sat here in her chair,
Smiling into the fire;
He who played stood there,
Bowing it higher and higher.

Childlike, I danced in a dream;
Blessings emblazoned that day;
Everything glowed with a gleam;
Yet we were looking away!

We tend to be "looking away" most of our lives, thinking of what comes next. Writing gives us a chance to look back, to put scenes and senses back together, to fill the gaps with the understanding that comes from hindsight.

The last exercise in this section offers a way of seeing ourselves again. I learnt it from the verse-novelist Bernadine Evaristo at a workshop. I have slightly adapted it here so that it can be done alone without workshop partners. It is in five short parts and should take about forty minutes.

Exercise

Begin with five minutes of automatic writing (see Chapter 1, Section 3) just to get warmed up. Take the following keywords and write for one minute on each:

Part 1

- House
- Photograph
- Voice
- Hair
- Kitchen

Don't read through what you have written. Put it aside and shut your eyes.

Part 2

You are a child again. See yourself as a child. Imagine you are looking at a cinema screen and seeing yourself as a child on film. What do you look like? Take a really good look at yourself, making a detailed mental note of everything you see. What are you wearing? Give the colours time to appear very distinctly. Describe the colours in your mind. How do your wear your hair? Did you always wear it like that, or was this some special occasion? What else is going on in the picture? Who else is there? Again, look at them very closely. Take plenty of time. Pay very exact attention to colours. And then to sounds. What can you hear? Voices? A door swinging open or shut? Describe these sounds to yourself as distinctly as possible. Then try to recapture smells. Can you smell food? Cooking? How does the room you are in smell? Or are you outside in the street? What smells can you notice? Can you smell your clothes? Or someone else's skin or breath? How do your clothes feel on your own skin?

Go on observing with your eyes shut. Keep your observations as concrete and as detailed as possible. If anyone walks in or out of the picture, make a very clear mental note of what they look like, what they are wearing, how they move. Take your time. Allow the picture to emerge in all its fullness.

When you are sure you have done full justice to the picture in your mind, open your eyes. Begin writing immediately. Write down, in painstaking detail, everything you have seen.

Part 3

Read your description through. Think a little about the child you have been looking at, your earlier self. Then write a letter to the

Part 4

person you were then from the person you are now. What is it that you most want to say to him or her? Address it as you would a normal letter, using your own name: Dear Richard ... With love, Richard. If there was a special nickname that you had in those days, you may want to use that.

Part 5

Now write a reply from your earlier self to your present self. Again, address it in the usual way, using your own name or nickname.

4 Plotting and Planning

Focus

So far, we have been looking at plot only in terms of the essential germ or central idea of your story. In this section we'll take a rather broader look at plot. Here, we'll be concerned with the overall structure of your story: where it is trying to go, and the stations it passes through in order to get there.

Knowing your Plot

It is absolutely essential to know exactly where you are trying to get to with your plot. It always helps to stand back from your ideas and ask yourself where they are all leading to. They may not be leading to any satisfying resolution or comforting conclusion, but even if your aim is to leave your reader hanging, this is still an aim, and you have to be very clear about it in your own mind. The reader has to believe at every stage of the journey that s/he is being taken somewhere worthwhile. Even if your ultimate intention is to disappoint the reader's expectations, you still have to make this very disappointment seem fundamentally worthwhile.

Types of Plot

One good way of gaining a clear and comprehensive sense of your plot is to try and typify it. What type of plot are you building? This involves breaking your story down to its bare essentials and comparing these to the essential constituents of other plots. There are various ways of doing this. One way is simply to ask yourself: what is desired in my story, and to what degree is this desire fulfilled? Consider the following possibilities.

- Character A lacks/desires entity/person B: does action X and gets B
- A lacks B: does X, but doesn't get B
- A lacks B: does X, but gets C and is inconsolable
- A lacks B: does X, but gets C and finds out that C is actually much better than B
- A lacks B: doesn't dare do X, so does Y; gets B all the same
- A lacks B: can't do X, so does Y; gets C and is inconsolable/delighted

Does your story more or less comform to any of these possibilities? Do you think it could be improved by adapting it to fit one of the others? The fourth possibility (A lacks B: does X, but gets C and finds out that C is actually much better than B) is, for very good reasons, a highly popular one. How many novels or stories can you think of which more or less fit this formula?

Narratives of Fortune

Another way of developing a clear sense of your plot and its basic direction is to think in terms of broader thematic prototypes. One such prototypical plot is the narrative of fortune. The legendary story of Dick Whittington (d. 1423), who, having failed to make his fortune, rests on Highgate Hill and hears the City bells calling out to him: "Turn again, Dick Whittington, Lord Mayor of London", is a classic example. CHARLES DICKENS draws on this story in several of his novels, including *Dombey and Son*, which follows not only Whittington-like Walter Gay's rise from wretchedness to wealth, but also Dombey's fall from riches to rags. Among DICKENS's other memorable fortune narratives are *David Copperfield* and *Great Expectations*. The "rags to riches" and "riches to rags" versions of the narrative of fortune are less popular today than they were in the nineteenth century, although elements of the fortune plot persist in nearly every Hollywood re-working of the American Dream.

Any story concerned with the endurance of adversity or the overcoming of an obstacle, however, will draw on the basic fortune topos, as is shown by countless modern narratives of war, imprisonment, deportation, and displacement. Both IMRE KERTÉSZ's Nobel-Prize-winning *Fateless* (1975) and IAN MCEWAN's *Atonement* (2001) are powerful examples of how the fortune plot has adapted itself to the needs and tastes of our own time.

Journey Narratives

There are hundreds of great journey narratives – from HOMER's *Odyssey* to FAULKNER's *As I Lay Dying*, from STERNE's *A Sentimental Journey through France and Italy* to JOYCE's one-day journey through Dublin in *Ulysses*. Journeys can be through time as well as space, and the landscapes they cover can be spiritual as well as material. What holds the reader's interest is how what happens on the way relates to the process of reaching a destination – even if the destination is never actually reached.

Do you have a journey story to write? Try jotting down a plan. Name the point of departure at the top of the page and put the destination at the bottom. Then start filling in the various places visited and things experienced on the way. Be on the lookout for journey narratives in your reading. Look at factual accounts as well as fictional ones.

Quest narratives are similar to journey narratives. The central difference is that here the journey involves the search for some-

Quest Narratives

thing specific. Classic examples of this are Holy Grail stories, such as *Parzifal* and *Gawain and the Green Knight*. A.S. BYATT'S *Possession* is a striking example of a more recent quest narrative, and much detective fiction is also based on key quest elements.

Quest stories are often about things that have gone missing, or secrets that beg to be revealed. The desire for revelation is a very strong motivation for a reader to read on. Even if you are not writing a quest narrative as such, you may want to incorporate a quest element into your story to stimulate a reader's interest. A long and detailed description of a place or a human activity can be made twice as compelling if there is a sense that it is leading up to some kind of revelation.

Narratives of Character

In plots in which character forms the centre of interest, ideas of fortune, journey and quest are all related to the internal development of the protagonist. These plots focus on processes of learning and recognition and the main interest lies not so much in what happens as in what the central character comes to realize. One classic form of the character narrative is the *Bildungsroman*, the novel of "education" in the broadest sense of the word. Novels like GOETHE'S *Wilhelm Meister* and ROUSSEAU'S *Emile* take as their focus the idea of "coming of age", but the basic recognition plot can turn on a much narrower (and less didactic) axis. JANE AUSTEN'S *Emma* is a story of character development through recognition, as are most of the novels of HENRY JAMES. Look at *What Maisie Knew* (1897) for an extraordinary representation of the gradual opening of a child's mind, or at *The Ambassadors* (1903) for JAMES'S own favourite analysis of the blossoming of a refined consciousness.

Reading for the Plot

We have looked at only four basic types of masterplot. There are, of course, many more. What other basic story-types can you think of? Get into the habit of abstracting the essential plot from the stories and novels you read. Is it a journey plot, a courtroom plot, a mistaken identity plot? Become more aware of the types of plot you especially like reading. Ask yourself why these plots particularly appeal to you. Also make a note of plot types that don't appeal to you. In the novel *Flaubert's Parrot* by JULIAN BARNES, the narrator gives a somewhat tongue-in-cheek list of plots he thinks ought to be banned. Here are a few examples:

There shall be no more novels in which a group of people, isolated by circumstances, revert to the "natural condition" of man, become essential, poor, bare, forked creatures... There is to be a twenty year ban on novels set in Oxford and Cambridge, and a ten year ban on other university fiction... No novels about small, hitherto forgotten wars in distant parts of the British Empire, in the painstaking course of which we learn first, that the British are averagely wicked; and secondly, that war is very nasty indeed ... No novels in which the narrator, or any of the characters, is identified simply by an initial letter. Still they go on doing it! (Flaubert's Parrot: 98–9)

As you become more conscious of plot, you will probably recognize that you do occasionally enjoy a book with a plot that was formerly on your banning list. This is an important recognition. Your taste in plot says many things about you. One of the things it should point out is that you have limitations begging to be challenged. Just as it is important to read widely in themes and styles that do not belong to your immediate sphere of tastes and interests, so it is important to write ourselves out of our familiar realms. Take one of the plot types on your blacklist and use it as the basis for a story. Be generous with the plot; give it a fair chance. You might just find the story works – maybe even better than the stories you thought you preferred to write.

Experimenting with Plot

⑤ Telling and Showing

In the Preface to his novel, *The Nigger of the Narcissus*, JOSEPH CONRAD wrote:

Seeing

My task which I am trying to achieve is, by the power of the written word to make you hear, to make you feel – it is, before all, to make you see.

There is a world of difference between writing that tells the reader what is going on and writing that actually shows it. Nowadays, most writers, and probably most readers, would respond approvingly to CONRAD'S enterprise. "Showing" would certainly seem to appeal more to modern tastes than "telling". There are good reasons why this should be the case, but before we go on to look at them, I'd like to make two points about "telling". First, telling has not always been so misprized. And secondly, telling still has an important place in contemporary writing.

The stories of the eighteenth century are full of telling. They have narrators who simply can't keep out of the fray, and just have to jump in to address the reader directly. We don't, however, love novels like STERNE'S *Tristram Shandy* or FIELDING'S *Tom Jones* any the less for this. Indeed, the telling is very much part of the fun. There is still plenty of telling in the narrative fiction of the nineteenth century. THACKERAY, TROLLOPE, DICKENS and GEORGE ELIOT are all great tellers, as well as great showers. The taste for showing is really a late nineteenth – early twentieth century development. It has a lot to do with the narrative method of HENRY JAMES. JAMES wanted fiction to resemble drama; everything should be presented scenically, as it is on stage, without long and cumbersome nar-

Telling

ratorial explanations. For JAMES, writers like TROLLOPE who went "behind" the characters and action of the story and offered explicit comments to the reader were breaking the fundamental faith in the integrity of the fictional world. "Dramatise! Dramatise! Dramatise!" wrote HENRY JAMES.

The Moral

The point of this little digression is to show that the preference for showing over telling is a historical one, rather than necessarily an aesthetic one. Whether we share it or not, we have to recognize this shift in taste as a historical fact. What this fact means for us as writers is basically that we cannot write in a telling mode without to some degree evoking a sense of the past. A story written today that begins with the words "Dear Reader" will inevitably resonate with echoes from the past. The reader is almost bound to begin reading the story as a kind of parody. So the moral is: tell by all means, but know what you are letting yourself in for when you start telling.

Showing

As we have said, all the great tellers of the past were also great showers. They were all masters of the art of making us *see*. This art is central to narrative. If a story can be summed up in one sentence, it hardly needs to be told as narrative fiction. As FLANNERY O'CONNOR wrote in an essay on "Writing Short stories":

A story is a way to say something that can't be said any other way, and it takes every word in the story to say what the meaning is. You tell a story because a statement would be inadequate. (O'CONNOR 1972: 96)

Similarly, if a character can be fully described to us through a list of explicit personality traits, that character really can't be very interesting. The art of showing is the art of letting a world of people and places and events unfold before a reader as if s/he were there in the middle, hearing the voices, watching the action.

Showing Character

In the opening paragraph of *Emma*, JANE AUSTEN tells us, very explicitly, a thing or two about her main character:

Emma Woodhouse, handsome, clever, and rich, with a comfortable home and happy disposition, seemed to unite some of the best blessings of existence; and had lived nearly twenty-one years in the world with very little to distress or vex her.

We only really get to know Emma Woodhouse, however, when we see her in action in the story that follows. The Emma that JANE AUSTEN *shows* us, in contrast to the Emma she simply *tells* us about at the beginning of the novel, is not altogether blessed, and the things which vex her most are the direct products of her own character.

In KATHERINE MANSFIELD'S short story "Miss Brill", we get to know a rather lonely, nosy old spinster who has a somewhat pompous and illusory view of the world around her. The narrator of the story never tells us these things directly. There is not even a direct physical description of Miss Brill in the story. All we are given are the character's thoughts, her actions and her reactions to others. Every Sunday, Miss Brill goes alone to the "Jardins Publiques" and watches people and listens in to their conversations. Here is Miss Brill listening to the band playing:

Now there came a little "flutey" bit – very pretty! – a little chain of bright drops. She was sure it would be repeated. It was; she lifted her head and smiled.

You can hear the way Miss Brill says "very pretty" inside her head, and you can see that awful, self-satisfied smile. Miss Brill repeatedly uses the word "little" in her thoughts to describe the world around her. The reader soon realises that this is because she feels – or tries to feel – superior to her environment. KATHERINE MANSFIELD wrote the following about the story in a letter of January 17th 1921:

In Miss Brill *I choose not only the length of every sentence, but even the sound of every sentence. I choose the rise and fall of every paragraph to fit her, and to fit her on that day at that very moment. After I'd written it I read it aloud – numbers of times – just as one would play over a musical composition – trying to get it nearer to the expression of Miss Brill – until it fitted her.*

This is what showing is all about: making every last detail of the writing contribute to the manifestation of character – or of place, or time, or mood.

As with other aspects of character, feelings can be presented explicitly or implicitly. You can say that characters are happy, sad, angry, weary, or you can show them doing something which implicitly suggests the way they are feeling to the reader. JULIA BELL gives a helpful example of the difference in her discussion of the use of abstract terms in *The Creative Writing Course Book*. She starts out with a rather abstract description of a character's emotion:

Showing and Feeling

She curled up on the bed. From deep down inside her came a pitiful cry for a love that wasn't there. It was lost to her. She thrashed herself about, trying to prevent herself from being engulfed. (BELL/MAGRS 2001: 44)

Then, she offers a way of suggesting this emotion through physical description:

She lay on the bed and curled up so tight her knees were pressing into her eye sockets.

It is crucial to become aware of these differences between showing and telling in your reading. Take a look, for example, at the first three paragraphs of JAMES JOYCE'S "Eveline". What is being told and what is being shown? What is Eveline's state of mind at the beginning of the story, and how do we know what she is feeling?

Telling as Showing

Often enough, a piece of explicit telling can have an implicit showing function at the same time. What one person tells us about someone else will often show us something about the teller. Look at the way the first-person narrator of GRAHAM SWIFT'S "Seraglio" speaks about his wife:

My wife is beautiful. She has a smooth, flawless complexion, subtle, curiously expressive eyebrows, and a slender figure. I think these were the things which made me want to marry her, but though they have preserved themselves well in eight years they no longer have the force of a motive. She looks best in very dark or very pale colours. She is fastidious about perfumes, and tends devotedly our garden in Surrey.

This is clearly a passage of telling when it comes to the wife, but showing when it comes to the implicit self-characterization of the husband.

Adjectives and Adverbs

Finally, always be on the lookout for superflous describing-words in your writing. An extra adjective can often turn a piece of perfectly suggestive showing into a piece of heavy-handed telling. Generally, the choice of the right noun or verb will leave a stronger impression than a string of adjectives or adverbs that explain the thing or action in question. In the sentence: "His hands trembled nervously", for example, the word "nervously" adds nothing. The trembling hands already *show* the reader that the character is nervous. There is no need to tell the reader as well. Or: "She walked out of the room determinedly" tells us something. "She strode out of the room" shows it.

Coda

I'd like to end this section on "telling" and "showing", and this first chapter on setting out to write short fiction, with four brief statements by writers writing at very different times and in very different styles. The first is from CHARLES DICKENS, giving advice to a fellow novelist; it is an illustration of just how important showing was to this great teller:

It strikes me that you constantly hurry your narrative (and yet without getting on) by telling it, in a sort of impetuous breathless way, in your own person, when the people should tell it and act it for themselves. My notion always is, that when I have made the people to play out the play, it is, as it were, their business to do it, and not mine... I don't want you, in a novel, to present yourself to tell such things, but I want the things to be there.

And here is HENRY JAMES, writing in his Notebook at the end of the nineteenth century:

I realize – none too soon – that the scenic method is my absolute and only salvation.

Finally, here is E.L. DOCTOROW, writing at the end of the twentieth century:

Good writing is supposed to evoke sensation in the reader – not the fact that it is raining, but the feeling of being rained upon.

3

CHAPTER Telling Stories: The Nuts and Bolts

Focus

So far we have mainly been exploring resources for generating stories. I hope that the exercises have produced ideas that you are keen to work with and develop. I also hope that you will go back to these exercises whenever you feel a need to tap more of your own resources.

Now we are going to look at some of the tools and techniques you will need to turn your story ideas into coherent and convincing pieces of writing. We'll focus first on *character, setting, voice* and *perspective*, then turn to ways of *beginning* and *ending* stories.

1 Character

What and Who

The first thing we usually ask of a story is: what's it about? The second thing is: who is it about? The two questions are fundamentally related. What happens in a story depends largely on the characters involved, and characters are defined first and foremost by what they do and by what happens to them.

It is useful to remember that the divisions between plot and character are, to some degree at least, artificial. As HENRY JAMES famously put it in "The Art of Fiction" (1884):

I cannot imagine composition existing in a series of blocks ... What is character but the determination of incident? What is incident but the illustration of character? ... It is an incident for a woman to stand up with her hand resting on a table and look at you in a certain way; or if it be not an incident I think it will be hard to say what it is. At the same time it is an expression of character. (JAMES 1963: 87–88)

This is as true today as it was in 1884. HILARY MANTEL, author of such novels as *Vacant Possession* and *Fludd*, has recently written:

If you make your characters properly they will simply do what is within them, they'll act out the nature that you have given them, and there – you'll find – you have your plot. (BOYLEN 1993: 38)

Creating Characters

Where do fictional characters come from? At one basic level, most characters are the products of real-life observation, composites of various aspects of people we have seen and known. Writers tend to be obsessive people-watchers. The novelist PAUL MAGRS has said: "If you want to write fiction it's often because you are nosy." He goes on:

You want to know about people. You want to know what makes them tick. You've spent most of your life listening to the way they talk, watching how they behave. They intrigue you, they madden you, they fascinate you. (BELL/MAGRS 2001: 104)

Some writers keep a special notebook for recording their observations about people. When they suddenly need for a story a failed jazz musician or a disillusioned Marxist who's just found Jesus, they leaf back through their notes to the paragraphs they'd scribbled after meeting Auntie Alice's second husband or Brian's new flatmate. Of course they just take the details they need and make up the rest. But even the made-up rest comes from somewhere – bits and pieces of observation or reading and the like.

Photo-fit

Putting together characters can often resemble the way the police build up an image of a suspect. They cobble together bits of photographs in order to produce a recognizable likeness – one person's nose, another's mouth, another's eyes, and so on. Sometimes just a chin or a pair of eyebrows you see on a bus is enough to suggest the beginnings of character.

But non-visual details can be just as important. The way someone answers the phone, blows their nose, or chuckles when they hear a joke. All these details can prove invaluable when you come to create characters. Combine the way that man you saw on the train touched his nose when he entered the carriage with the way your cousin flicks her hair behind her ears and the way the woman at the shoeshop says "well it said size eight on the box," and what have you got?

Photo Albums

You probably know the feeling of being bored to distraction while a friend or relative shows you the third album stuffed with holiday snaps they took of their friends and relatives on Ibiza. Try imagining that you're looking through a catalogue of potential characters for your writing. Photographs can be very suggestive. Once you realize that leafing through a gallery of total strangers can be a valuable resource for writing, any photo album can become a potential treasure trove. Look out for faces that interest you. Put them in different situations, imagining the things they'd do or say. You are already creating fictional characters.

Get your friends to show you pictures of themselves as children. Ask yourself how the face and body you see could possibly have turned into the person you now know. Or pick up one of those old photographs you can often buy at flea markets and sit down in a café and invent an episode out of the person's life. You never know when just that person and just that episode may come in handy.

Names

Names can often be no less suggestive than faces. My mother has an amazing store of names from stories from her youth. There's Mr. Tullock, the rough and ready rugby coach from the boarding school where she once worked, who took a rather too lively interest in little boys, or the Right Reverend Sidebottom, who insisted on pronouncing his name "Siddybotóme". HENRY JAMES used to scan the columns of *The Times* for names and jotted them down in his notebooks. Lots of them ended up in his novels and short stories. His use of the name Capadose for a mendacious old general in the short story "The Liar" actually induced an inquiry from a member of a family of that name. He replied somewhat apologetically in a letter that was printed in Isaäc Da Costa's *Noble Families Among the Sephardic Jews*. One could write a nice story about the uncanny experience of a character who comes across his name in a piece of fiction and finds a hidden aspect of his personality revealed.

Your Name

Think about your own name, both your first name and your surname. Where do they come from, what do they mean? There is, inevitably, a story in every family name.

How do you feel about your name? Does it suit you? This is also a question you can ask of your characters. Do they feel at home in the names you've given them? Not long ago, I visited the loo on a German train and someone outside started knocking at the door, calling my name. It was a woman's voice, pronouncing my name perfectly in English. I opened the door to a complete stranger. She apologized in German and walked off down the corridor. Hearing one's name can be a pretty uncanny experience.

Getting to Know your Characters

You will have to know your characters very well to give your reader the chance to know them even a little. That is, you need to know more about your characters than you ever say in your story. Your story will offer no more than a thinnish slice of your character's life. But what goes into that slice are the quirks and habits, the phobias and desires, the agony and the ecstasy of a whole human being. You need to have the whole picture in order to carve off a convincing slice.

Portfolios

Try to build up as full a picture of your character as possible. Remember, the material you don't actually use in your story will be as important as the details you do use. Never say to yourself: I don't really need to know this, after all, it won't appear in the story. The story is just the tip of the iceberg when it comes to characterization. The character who walks onto the stage of a short story has already to be a full and living being in your mind.

Keep a file on every character you intend to write about. Keep adding to it over time. When you overhear a conversation between a mother and daughter and think to yourself: that's just what my character might say to her mother – add the phrase to your file. If you see a pair of shoes you can imagine your character wearing, write down a description and add it to your file.

Keep going until you have a full character portfolio that you can draw on when you come to write. It is, of course, for you to decide what kind of information this portfolio should contain, but here are a few suggestions that you may find helpful.

Appearance

You may or may not wish to describe your character's physical appearance in your story. In any case, write a one-page physical description of your character. This is for you. If you don't have a pretty clear idea of how your characters look, it will be even harder for your readers to visualize them.

Go into as much detail as possible. Describe their clothes; clothes say a lot about people. Where do your characters buy their clothes? Are clothes important to them? How do they wear their hair? Do they always wear it the same, or do they change it according to different moods and occasions?

Habits

Think first about habits that relate directly to a character's appearance. Does s/he smoke? If so, how? There is a world of difference between someone who holds a cigarette between forefinger and thumb and someone who snaps back their wrist, splaying two fingers into a broad "V". Does your character take long drags or short puffs? Does s/he blow smoke rings? Do you have a mental picture of the smoke-ring-blowing type?

Try to think of other details that reveal something about a person on a first encounter. Try describing habitual gestures your characters make with their hands, the way they put on or take off their (sun)glasses, or the way they nibble their knuckles while reading a book.

Then go on to more general habits. Think of things your characters do every day or every week, or on the first Sunday of every month. What do these things tell you about your characters? Again, all you are trying to do is to get to know your creatures better. The more details you have, the better you will know your character and, regardless of how much detail you actually use in the story, the more convincing your character will be.

Voice

How does your character speak? Try writing half a page of direct speech in your character's voice. Does your character have a particular accent? Are there certain words or types of words, or turns of phrase s/he uses often? Your characters may not actually speak once in your story, but you may none the less try to suggest their voices when describing their thoughts and reactions.

How do they tell stories? Have them retell the story of a book they've just read or a film they've just seen. Is that how you would

tell a story? Listen to the way your friends tell stories, and borrow some of their patterns and mannerisms where appropriate.

Try experimenting with how your characters speaks to different people. Do their voices change? Do they have a telephone voice, for example, or an in-the-pub-with-the-lads voice? Try having dialogues with them. Ask them questions and let them respond in their own voices.

Situations

How do your characters react in different situations? Sit one in a taxi, stuck in a traffic jam, on the way to an important appointment. Have another run into an old schoolfriend at a bus stop. How do they respond when they are told they haven't got the job they applied for? How do they celebrate their birthdays?

Also, ask yourself what your characters feel about issues that are potentially important to them but don't necessarily get mentioned in your story. How do they feel about having children, about where they're from, about their father's second marriage? Think about issues that are particularly relevant to their lives, but also experiment with less obvious questions. Would they travel to the moon if given a chance?

What are your characters' wildest dreams? What are their most terrible fears? Try to write down at least one dream your main character has had.

Possessions

Picture your character's house. Go into the living room and look at all the odds and ends on the mantelpiece. Sneak into the bedroom and make a note of what's on the bedside table. If your character was sent to live on a desert island, what would s/he take along, what couldn't s/he possibly live without? What are you likely to find in your character's pockets or handbag on any ordinary day of the week? Make a list, and think about what this list tells you.

Lists

Lists of this kind can be very useful. Experiment with other lists. Try a shopping list, for example. What does your character buy and where? Does s/he get everything from the supermarket, or go to the butcher's for meat, the greengrocer's for fresh fruit, etc.? Write a "to do" list for your character. List the items in order of urgency. Make up other lists that reveal something important about your character.

Conflict

Most "real" characters are, in one way or another, in conflict with themselves. There are things they'd love to do, but don't dare. They feel guilty about something they've done, but can't talk about it. They always fall for the same people, even though they know they shouldn't. Think about the conflicts that both motivate and restrain your characters. Where do they come from? Their family? The expectations of others? What situations are likely to trigger off conflicts within your characters? What situations are going to bring them into conflict with others? Who is the most dangerous person for your main character to come into contact with?

Finally, try living in your character's skin for a while. Sit down with your notebook in the evening and think of all the things that have happened to you during the day. Respond to them not as yourself, but as if you were your character. Write in the first person, again trying to imitate your character's voice as closely as possible.

Being your Character

Keep plugging away at these exercises until you know your character inside out. Come back to them whenever you get stuck while writing, whenever you're not sure how your character should react or where s/he should go next.

2 Setting

Whenever we read stories, we automatically start building a mental picture of the physical world in which they are set. We want a sense of place and feel frustrated, cheated if we don't get it. Good writing gives us a very vivid sense of place. Look at the opening of ELIZABETH BOWEN'S short story "Mysterious Kôr":

Where?

Full moonlight drenched the city and searched it; there was not a niche left to stand in. The effect was remorseless: London looked like the moon's capital – shallow, cratered, extinct. It was late, but not yet midnight; now the buses had stopped the polished roads and streets in this region sent for minutes together a ghostly unbroken reflection up. The soaring new flats and the crouching old shops looked equally brittle under the moon, which blazed in windows that looked its way. The futility of the black-out became laughable: from the sky, presumably, you could see every slate in the roofs, every white curb, every contour of the naked winter flower-beds in the park; and the lake, with its shining twists and tree-darkened islands would be a landmark for miles, yes, miles, overhead.

This picture of London is highly memorable, not only because it is vivid, but also because it is strange. The reason for the strangeness only gradually becomes clear, and by then a description of place has already become an evocation of time, set in a readily identifiable story of war.

Become a compulsive collector of locations. Use your notebook like a sketchpad and jot down descriptions of places you find yourself in. Any place will do. You can simply never tell when you are going to need a particular location in your future writing. Make quick verbal sketches at the bus stop, on a station platform, in cafés, looking out of your window onto the street at night. These

Sketching

descriptions needn't resemble anything like polished prose. Just a few phrases, like brushstrokes, to trigger your memory of a particular scene.

It's useful to date these sketches. Six months later, you may find yourself writing a story that involves a meeting in a laundry. When was it that you sat in that laundry at night watching a man emptying all the machines to look for his own washing? It was still light, so it must have been summer. So you leaf through your notebooks for entries dated July.

Place and Plot

You can also use these sketches of place to kickstart stories. Start writing up one of your sketches and put a character in it who doesn't obviously belong there. Perhaps, when thinking about characterization, you made a character sketch of your rather posh landlord. Put him in your laundry setting. What's he doing there? What's happened to him? Questions like these might lead you to an altogether different story. Of a woman, say, who suddenly decides to stop washing her husband's clothes. It can still begin with a picture of the husband sitting in the laundry at night, utterly dejected.

Place and Person

Place is intimately related to person. It is nearly always a form of characterization. The backdrops we set our characters in tell us something about them. If they don't, descriptions of place run the risk of being merely decorative.

Think about the spaces your characters spend most of their time in. Do they return at night to an unmade bed? Is the living room carpet so meticulously hoovered that you'd hardly dare tread on it? Do they ask you to take your shoes off when you come into their houses? Are there pink fluffy slippers waiting for them by the door? What knick-knacks do they have on the mantlepiece. Do they have wallpaper that speaks to you – and does it shout or whisper?

Exercise

Write a description of the room you spend most of your time in. Write it as a kind of self-portrait, only without mentioning yourself explicitly. Let the objects in the room speak for you, speak about you.

Try this with friends' rooms too. See if you can characterize friends and acquaintances just by describing the spaces and things among which they move.

Be discreetly nosy when you visit other people's houses. Take mental notes of the relationships between people and things. Never decline an offer of the perennial "tour" of the flat or house. You might just see something you need: exactly the right bed for your character to wake up in in a strange apartment, or just the type of linen cupboard s/he hid in as a child.

Home, as always, is a good place to start gathering ideas and images about setting. If you can develop a strong awareness of how you are related to your own physical environment and background, you will find it easier to do the same for your fictional characters. In what ways do you carry around with you a house, a street, a town, a community, a landscape? Let's take these settings one by one. First think and write about your own background, then go back and do the same for a fictional character.

Home

Think of the various houses and flats you have lived in during your life. Choose one that is particularly important for you. It may be the house you were born in, or it may be where you live now.

Do a gradual tour of the house. If you still live there, walk around like a complete stranger, noticing every detail. Ask yourself what kind of person lives here. If you no longer live in the house or apartment, do the tour in your head. Wander very slowly from room to room, taking time to let the full picture emerge. As always pay attention to sounds and smells as well as the way things look. All homes have a particular smell. It's often the first thing we notice when visiting friends or strangers. Most blocks of flats also have a distinctive smell. You smell it in the hall and on the stairs. Try to find words for these smells. How do they relate to the people you're writing about? If you no longer perceive any distinctive smell in your own block or flat or house, ask a friend to describe it to you with an outsider's nose.

A Stranger in the House

Now go out into the street – either in reality or in your mind. Make verbal sketches of everything you see. Look at shop windows and go into the shops. Listen to conversations, make a mental note of the butcher's apron, or the old lady who's always in a muddle with her change. Are there characters you always see on the street? Let your imagination run free with their stories.

Try going out into the street at different times of the day, especially times when you're usually indoors. What is the street like at five in the morning or in the middle of the night? Does it have a different feel mid-morning and mid-afternoon? This may be something you can use. The change of atmosphere might reflect or clash with the mood of your character at different points in the day.

The Street

Get to know your town, its layout, its history. What kind of people live there, what kind of work is there for them? Are you a true child of your town, or were you always an outsider?

Again, walk around town like a stranger, saying to yourself "that's funny, that's odd". Stop at buildings you pass every day and ask yourself when they were built, who by, who for. Look in through the windows and imagine who lived there once and who

The Town

lives there now. Look into the past of some of the lesser known landmarks.

Are there parks and playgrounds in your town? Who goes there and what do they get up to? If there's a swimming pool, go and sit up in the gallery. It can be a great place to write, with the backdrop of splashing and echoing voices.

Landscape Get out of town and explore the country that surrounds it. Get to know its contours, its weather, its winds. Do you feel this landscape inside you? What does it mean to you when you return to the hills, valleys, plains, marshlands, copses, watermeadows of home?

How are people related to the landscapes in which they live or from which they come? How does the lie of the land affect our spirits and everyday lives? For a wonderful example of the fictional evocation of landscape, have a look at GRAHAM SWIFT'S novel *Waterland* (1983), set in the Fens of East Anglia. Swift once said in an interview that many readers of the book were very surprised to learn that the author was not actually from the Fens himself, but from London.

③ Who Speaks?

Voice When you start reading a piece of fiction, you can generally hear a voice speaking to you. The voice in a story by PHILIP ROTH will be very different from that in a story by KATHERINE MANSFIELD or CHARLES DICKENS. What kind of person do you want to tell your story? How does s/he *sound*? Do you want to tell your story in your own voice, or do you want to suggest the speech-style of someone else – one of your characters, perhaps?

Story-tellers There are as many types of story-teller as there are different types of story. There is the tight-lipped narrator who gives nothing but the facts – no fancy description, no paperback psychology. And there is the garrulous narrator who just can't stop talking, and comments on every last detail of the story. There are narrators who clearly symphathise with their characters, narrators who hate them, and narrators who remain entirely neutral. There are narrators who appear in the story as characters and tell the whole thing in the first person, and there are narrators who stay well out of it all and take an all-knowing bird's-eye view.

Think carefully about what kind of narrator best suits the story you want to tell. Once you have made your choice, you will need to be consistent. You can't have a narrator describing a character both as "he" and "I", and you can't have a narrator knowing everything one minute and nothing the next. I'm sorry, let me rephrase that: you *can* do these things, but you need to have a damned good reason. It has to be part of your basic plan. Otherwise it will simply come across as shoddy workmanship.

We'll be looking at the use of different narrators in more detail in the next chapter. For now, it might be helpful just to read a handful of short stories and to compare the types of narrator that tell them, and the voices in which they speak. Try to be very aware of these issues every time you read a piece of fiction. Have a look, for example, at the following stories and compare their narrative voices: EDGAR ALLAN POE, "The Murders in the Rue Morgue", VIRGINIA WOOLF, "Kew Gardens", D.H. LAWRENCE "Fanny and Annie", DORIS LESSING, "To Room Nineteen", TRUMAN CAPOTE, "A Christmas Memory", GRAHAM SWIFT, "Seraglio".

Examples

4 Who Sees?

The question of "who sees?" in a story is as important as "who speaks". And the answer is by no means necessarily the same. Narrators can perceive the events of a story through their own eyes or through the eyes of one or more characters. In JAMES JOYCE'S very short story "Eveline", for example, the world presented is seen through Eveline's eyes, although she is clearly not the person narrating the story. In NICK HORNBY'S *About a Boy*, the narrator narrates one chapter from the point of view of Marcus, a twelve-year-old boy, and the next from that of Will, who's thirty-six. In HENRY JAMES'S *What Maisie Knew*, the action of the whole novel is presented through the very limited perspective of a little girl who gradually understands more and more of what is going on.

Point-of-View

Perspective in a story is rather like the lens of the camera in a film. It is the point of view through which all information is filtered. This point of view can of course change. The camera can alternate between several perspectives. When you write a story, you will need to decide on the point of view from which you want to tell it. Restricting the perspective to that of a single main character can give enormous insight into that character's mind. But if you go for a single perspective, you will have to be careful not to relate any information that is beyond your character's knowledge. Again, you can mix and play with perspectives, but you have to know what you are doing and why you are doing it.

A Lens

We'll be doing more detailed work on perspective in the next chapter. Try to identify the point of view from which stories are told whenever you read them. Does the perspective change? Does the narrative style also change when a new character-point-of-view is introduced?

Examples

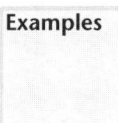

Have a look, for starters, at the following stories: D.H. LAWRENCE, "The Rocking Horse Winner", JAMES JOYCE, "Eveline", V. S. PRITCHETT, "A Family Man", ALAN SILLITOE, "The Fishing Boat Picture", BERNARD MAC LAVERTY, "Words the Happy Say".

⑤ Beginnings

Importance

Precisely because short stories are short, the beginning inevitably makes up a larger proportion of the text than is the case in longer forms of narrative fiction. For this reason, the beginning of a short story is extremely important.

Doorways

The beginning is a doorway into the story. It has to be inviting if you want to draw your reader in. There is no simple recipe for doing this, but it definitely helps to be aware of what you are doing and why you are doing it. Are you introducing a character, setting a scene, evoking a mood, or simply plunging the reader into the middle of a gripping story? Whatever you are doing, you will want to arouse the reader's curiosity. The reader has to want to know what will happen next.

Direction

Beginnings have to know where they are going. A detailed description of objects that will play no major role in the story is probably going to be both a waste of space and a loss of focus. In a short story, every detail has to be made to count. Why is the knife you've just described important? Will it reappear later as the murder-weapon? Even a copious description of apparently irrelevant details *can* be important: if it tells us something essential about the way a character looks at the world, for example. But you have to know where the story is heading before you write those opening sentences. Everything you say in them must lead towards the climax that is to come.

Hearing Ahead

The conductor, WILHELM FURTWÄNGLER, described a similar process in performing a piece of music. He used the term *Fernhören*, "far-hearing" or "hearing ahead," to describe the way in which he tried, in the opening bars of a symphony, to give a premonition of what was to come, preparing the listener's ear for the unfolding drama.

Begin Last

In order to do this, of course, the writer, like the conductor of an orchestra, has to know what's coming in advance. Know the whole story before you allow yourself to fall in love with an opening sentence. Know the details that are going to be important, the twists and turns that can already be latently suggested from the start. Often enough, of course, the opening of a story is the first idea we have: a scene, an action, a sentence. That first sentence may end up being just perfect; but always go back to it, openmindedly and critically, when the rest of the story is there.

Types of
Beginnings

In *The Way to Write Short Stories* (1986), MICHAEL BALDWIN insisted that beginnings should suggest one of three things:

"a. *Something of moment is about to happen or is already happening ...* b. *We are being initiated into a fascinating world ...* c. *We are suspending our need for a and b because this writer is so engagingly witty.*

There is no end to the variety of ways in which writers achieve these ends, and the best way of exploring them is to read widely and get into the habit of noticing the opening strategies different writers employ. For the moment, however, let's take a look at six basic types of short story beginnings that have been widely and effectively used.

In medias res

Most stories don't begin at the beginning. Something has already happened. Sometimes it isn't clear exactly what has happened, and the reader has to work it out. This is one way of drawing the reader in: making him or her ask questions that can only be answered by reading on. JOHN BURNSIDE's short story "Kate's Garden", for example, begins: *"The day Tom Williams came back I was still working at home."* We are faced with the obvious questions of the identity of Tom Williams and the significance of his return, but also that little "still" in the second half of the sentence makes us wonder what the narrator did at home, why he stopped working there, and where he went on to work.

Further
Examples

Look at the first two sentences of ERNEST HEMINGWAY's "The Battler": *"Nick stood up. He was all right"*. Who is Nick? What has happened to him? The third sentence already offers us a clue: *"He looked up at the track at the lights of the caboose going out of sight around the curve."* But to know more, we have to read on.

Here are some more examples of beginnings that leave the reader needing to go on in order to answer questions:

"By seven thirty they were ready to go." FAY WELDON, "Weekend". Who was ready, we ask; and to go where?

"And after all, the weather was ideal." KATHERINE MANSFIELD, "The Garden Party". Here, the reader is plunged into the middle of a character's thoughts. Who is thinking this? For what was the weather ideal?

"Thomas withdrew to the side of the window and with his head between the wall and the curtain he looked down on the driveway where the car had stopped." FLANNERY O'CONNOR, "The Comforts of Home". Who is Thomas, why is he looking out of the window so furtively, and who has just arrived? This last question is answered by the second sentence, which only goes on to raise questions of its own. *"His mother and the little slut were getting out of it."* Who is the "lit-

tle slut"? Is this Thomas's view of her, and if so why does he see her like that? Already we're drawn into a story of considerable emotional charge.

Setting

Stories often begin by creating a sense of place. We have already looked at the importance of place and setting in this chapter. Have another look at the excerpt from ELIZABETH BOWEN'S "Mysterious Kôr" for the use of setting at the beginning of a story. Note the way that place is already bound up with both atmosphere and plot. Description always needs to be functional at the beginning of a story. You are trying to get the reader into the story as quickly and effectively as possible. You can use the description of place to set the tone of your story and even to introduce certain motifs.

Example

In the opening of his short story "Chemistry", GRAHAM SWIFT makes a very careful and suggestive use of setting:

The pond in our park was circular, exposed, perhaps fifty yards across. When the wind blew, little waves travelled across it and slapped the paved edges, like a miniature sea.

This sounds simple enough, but when we read on we discover just how carefully chosen this beginning is. The idea of the "miniature sea" is important both because the pond becomes a kind of micro-cosm in the story and because we learn later that the narrator's father "disappeared without a trace" into the sea. The story is in many ways itself "circular" – it ends, for one thing, back down at the pond – and the narrator is an "exposed" character. The waves travelling across the pond anticipate other images of travel in the story, and the exposed geometry of the pond is in tune with the "sad symmetry" of the relations the story describes.

Character

Short stories often begin with a piece of characterization. This can be quite general and direct, as in the opening sentence of JOYCE CARY'S "The Breakout": *"Tom Sponson, at fifty-three, was a thoroughly successful man."* But it can also be a lot more specific, as in the opening of KATHERINE MANSFIELD'S "The Singing Lesson":

With despair – cold, sharp despair – buried deep in her heart like a wicked knife, Miss Meadows, in cap and gown and carrying a little baton, trod the cold corridors that led to the music hall.

Here, character is already bound up with story and situation. Read the stories of FLANNERY O'CONNOR for exemplary beginnings that situate characters in telling modes of behaviour. Here are just three sample beginnings from her stories:

Examples

Old Dudley folded into the chair he was gradually molding to his own shape and looked out the window fifteen feet into another window framed by blackened red brick. "The Geranium"

Hazel Motes walked along downtown, close to the storefronts but not looking at them. His neck was thrust forward as if he were trying to smell something that was always being drawn away. "The Peeler"

Enoch Emery knew when he woke up that today the person he could show it to was going to come. He knew it by his blood. He had wise blood like his daddy. "The Heart of the Park"

First-Person

A first-person self-characterization can also be a very effective way of beginning a story. Many writers use the first-person voice ironically, establishing at once with the reader a shared distance from the voice of the narrating "I". We have already seen an instance of this in IAN MCEWAN's "Dead as They Come". A similar effect is achieved by ROSE TREMAIN in the opening of "My Wife is a White Russian":

I am a financier. I have financial assets, world-wide. I'm in nickel and pig-iron and gold and diamonds. I like the sound of all these words. They have an edge, I think. The glitter of saying them sometimes gives me an erection.

An excellent example of the use of first-person self-characterization at the beginning of a short story is GRAHAM SWIFT's "Seraglio". The first paragraph of SWIFT's story is worth quoting in full and analyzing in some detail:

Example

In Istanbul there are tombs, faced with calligraphic designs, where the dead Sultan rests among the tiny catafalques of younger brothers whom he was obliged, by custom, to murder on his accession. Beauty becomes callous when it is set beside savagery. In the grounds of the Topkapi Palace the tourists admire the turquoise tiles of the Harem, the Kiosks of the Sultans, and think of girls with sherbet, turbans, cushions, fountains. 'So were they just kept here?' my wife asks. I read from the guide-book: 'Though the Sultans kept theoretical power over the Harem, by the end of the sixteenth century these women effectively dominated the Sultans.'

Comment

This opening paragraph initially appears to be a fairly objective description of tombs in Istanbul. Only towards the end of the passage do we realise that it is a piece of first-person narration that actually says a good deal about the character of the narrator, his wife, and their relationship. The narrator is the type of man who answers his wife's questions by reading from a guide-book. The paragraph is, moreover, an extraordinary example of narrative *Fernhören* or "hearing ahead". The whole story turns out to be about the intimate relationship between beauty and savagery. Note the words "calligraphic" and "callous". "Calligraphy" – beautiful handwriting – is from the Greek *kallos*, meaning beauty. Callous is from Latin *callus*, meaning hard, particularly as in "hard skin". The roots of these two words encapsulate the essential opposition of the story. They are also words from two different historical cultures, and the meeting of historical cultures is another central theme of the story. Finally, the last sentence employs the rhetorical figure of the chiasmus – the crossing of elements in a sentence in the form: AB:BA. This structure is itself central to the story that will be told: a story about power relations between men and women. The figure of the chiasmus comes up again later on: "Men want power over women in order to be able to let women take this power from them." Everything about the opening of SWIFT's "Seraglio" is finely crafted to have bearing on what is to follow. Try to demand as much from your beginnings as SWIFT clearly does from his.

Dialogue

Dialogue is character in action. Many short stories begin with dialogue or direct speech. This can draw the reader into the story in several different ways at once. On the one hand, a snippet of speech is always *in medias res*, a response to something else that has already happened or been said. On the other hand, speech is always also characterization; it tells us something about the person speaking. We already get to know quite a bit about Harry and Brenda through the opening snippets of conversation in DAVID LODGE's "Hotel des Boobs":

"Hotel des Pins!" said Harry. "More like Hotel des Boobs."
"Come away from that window," said Brenda. "Stop behaving like a peeping Tom."

Speech can also be story in action. Take the opening of ALDOUS HUXLEY's "The Gioconda Smile":

"Miss Spence will be down directly, sir"'
"Thank you," said Mr Hutton, without turning round.

One person is waiting for another. We are not told this; it is simply enacted by the spoken exchange. We also register the detail that Mr Hutton doesn't turn round, and already want to know what this says about him and his current state of mind.

Or, for a more dramatic example of speech as action, look at the beginning of "The Giant Woman" by JOYCE CAROL OATES:

"Get away! Get away! Get out of here!"
She came at us, swinging something. It struck the side of the shed – there was a metallic sound – and then her screaming again.
" – out of here – I'll kill –"
The others were ahead of me. I ran, whimpering with fear.

Direct speech can also be a good eye-catcher at the beginning of a story, as in "The Lotus" by JEAN RHYS: "Garland says she's a tart." A sentence like this can arouse interest in both the speaker and the person spoken of – while also, of course, leaving us wondering: who is Garland?

Some stories begin very effectively by bringing two different elements together and making the reader wonder what the connection is. In this way, they are rather like Haiku poems (see Chapter 7), which often bring two apparently unrelated images together and then offer a third which makes sense of them. An example might go something like this:

Haiku Beginnings

Three shots rang out in the valley. On the hillside Logan went on inspecting his vines. Now and then he lifted a fat cluster of grapes to his lips and imparted the gentlest of kisses.

What, the reader wants to know, does Logan have to do with the shots that have been fired? Perhaps it will turn out that he has ordered someone's execution. ADAM THORPE does something similar at the beginning of his story "The First Day": *"He called me when the rains cleared. The mountains lost their grey hoods and smiled."* He then goes on describing the mountains and their forests, and doesn't come back to the call until the next paragraph. This kind of delay or displacement inevitably raises tension.

The opening of SARAH MAY'S "Blueprint" is haikuesque in a rather different way:

Holding an umbrella in one hand, and his briefcase open between his legs, Klaus Konditorei started to feel his way through the rubbish bin, layer after layer, moved as always to tears.

The juxtaposition of civil servant (which is what Klaus is) and rubbish bin is a surprise in itself, but the "moved as always to tears" opens a whole new range of meaning. We are left asking not only what is a civil servant doing rummaging in a rubbish bin, but why does he "always" do this and what is behind the emotion that he always feels? There is clearly a whole story in this brief juxtaposition of images: a story that would be worth having even if it simply stopped after the first sentence.

The point of the beginning of a story is to get the reader hooked. One effective way of doing this is with a particularly striking first sentence, or opening cluster of sentences. This can begin as a general statement about the world, such as the opening sentence of GRAHAM SWIFT'S "The Son":

Eye-Catchers

It's true: everything changes. What you think you know, you don't know. What's good or bad at one time isn't good or bad at another. Once I cut off the fingers of my own mother.

Or take the opening of "The Watch" by the same author: *"Tell me, what is more magical, more sinister, more malign yet consoling, more expressive of the constancy – and fickleness – of fate than a clock?"* An eye-catching opening can also be a statement about the story to be told. FORD MADDOX FORD began his novel *The Good Soldier* with the sentence: *"This is the saddest story I've ever heard."* Or it can simply be a rather surprising formulation, like the first sentence of MARTIN AMIS'S "Let me Count the Times": *"Vernon made love to his wife three and a half times a week, and this was all right."* What all these openings have in common is that they leave the reader intrigued and wanting to know more.

6 Finishing

Know What you're Doing

It is both hard and risky to offer advice about how to end a story. There are certainly no neat formulas that one can draw on. Everything depends on exactly what it is you're trying to do. If your story is above all a slice of life, or the depiction of a small and unremarkable moment in a person's life, then it would be odd to end with a momentous turn of events. If you've started by suggesting there's a secret to be revealed, you will frustrate your readers if you fail to reveal it by the end. This may, however, be exactly the effect you're after – especially if you're writing a garden-path story. The main thing is to know what you're doing – and to know it, and give the reader the sense that you know it, from the very first sentence.

As always, the best way to develop an informed sense of the possibilities of story-endings is to read widely and consciously. Note down endings you feel work well and try to ask yourself why they work. (BERNARD MALAMUD is a master story-ender. Pick up any of his volumes of stories and just read the endings one by one). Be equally attentive to endings you find unsatisfactory; is it that they are lacking something, or do they try to do too much?

Back to the Beginning

Many stories end by returning to their own point of departure. This can create a sense of completion without needing any additional narrative twist. Another possibility worth exploring is a return not so much to the content of the beginning, as to its mode. Even if you choose not to do this, it is still worth thinking about setting, character, dialogue and statement as potential ending modes. And stories can end in mid-air just as well as beginning *in medias res*.

CHAPTER 4 Telling a Story Again

1 Preparation

Focus

In this chapter we are going to write one story in several different ways. We shall be keeping the story very simple, and varying the ways in which it is told according to time, perspective and style. The purpose of the chapter is twofold: first, to practise a series of different story-telling techniques, and second, to work on critical distance. You will have to get used to starting all over again and rewriting from new angles and with new aims.

It's inevitable that details of your story will change with every rewriting. Don't try to prevent this. Writing the same story for the umpteenth time will get boring unless you allow different approaches to inject new ideas, new twists in the plot. In any piece of writing, the aim is always to end up having more than you started with.

Suggestion

I suggest you take this chapter very slowly. It contains, taken at regular intervals, about two weeks' work. Once you have got the basic version of your story ready, aim to write one new version a day. Set yourself a time when you are going to have a go at one of the exercises and try to return to them at the same time every day. It is of course quite possible to do several rewrites at a single sitting, but it is probably better to give the story a rest. This will also help you to create a distance from what you have done – which is in any case half the point.

Automatic Writing

We will begin with a simple automatic writing exercise. Take the following four keywords:

- Railway station
- Door
- Secret
- Window

Write for two minutes on each word. Remember, once you have started writing, you must not pause for thought or lift your pen from the page. Write as quickly as you can, and, as soon as the two minutes have passed, move on to the next keyword without completing your last sentence.

When you have written on all four keywords, read through what you have done. Circle ten words that interest you. Seven should be nouns, and three verbs. Write these ten words down on a separate piece of paper. We shall come back to them in a moment.

Characters

Invent three characters. You can draw upon the characters you created in the last chapter or create new ones. One character has a secret. The second knows that the first has a secret, but can only guess at what it is. The third character knows nothing at all about the secret. Keep the characters fairly simple. You only need write a profile of about half a page on each. You should give your characters proper names. For the purposes of the exercise, however, we shall call them A, B, and C.

Story

Now write a story around the ten words you selected from the Automatic Writing exercise. All ten words have to appear in the story. Create three basic story elements: a beginning, a middle, and an end. Use the idea of the minimal plot discussed in Chapter 2 ("Plotting and Planning"). That is: there is a task to accomplish, the attempt to accomplish it, and the results of the attempt. In this case we will make the pattern a bit more specific:

Someone wants to do something in order to change their situation. They do it, but it only partly works. Their situation is changed, but not exactly as they had intended.

Thus, we have a wish, an action, and a consequence. This is your basic storyline.

Outline

When you have worked out the three basic elements of the story, think of a keyword or phrase to characterize each element. Above the keyword or phrase, draw a simple geometrical figure like a square, a circle, or a triangle. For example:

$$\square \qquad \bigcirc \qquad \triangle$$

A. has secret;   lies to B;   in trouble with C.

These figures will symbolize the basic building blocks of your story.

Time

The time-frame for your story will be 24 hours.

Length

Now you have the basic ingredients for a very short story. As you are going to be rewriting it several times, do remember to keep it short. It really shouldn't be more than three pages of A4, and could even be considerably shorter. Also, before you go on to the next stage, make sure the story really interests you, as you will be working with the same ideas now for the next few days.

2 Versions of the Story

1. Perspective

It's time to begin the first of several versions of your story. Try to write the story as objectively as possible, in the third person, from the point of view of an all-seeing and all-knowing narrator. This narrator has no axe to grind and no pet favourites in the story. S/he simply presents the events, actions, and the speech and thoughts of the characters as clearly and simply as possible. Write in short, concise sentences. This version of the story should be little more than a skeleton of the basic ideas. The flesh and blood we'll be adding later.

A Bird's-eye View

Now write a second version of the same story from the perspective of Character A. You should continue to write in the third person; i.e., your narrator is not the character him- or herself, but a storyteller who does not appear as a character in the story, and yet who presents everything that happens from the point of view of Character A.

Focus 1

Notice that there may be some details in your first version of the story that cannot be reproduced in this second version. Character A may not perceive everything that happens in the story. There may be certain things that s/he doesn't know about. Nevertheless, keep the point of view of this version of the story restricted to the perspective of Character A. Only narrate information that Character A can reasonably be assumed to know or to have perceived. Present to the reader Character A's reactions to the events narrated. Feel free to present Character A's thoughts. Where there are things s/he doesn't know, it is perfectly reasonable to let her or him speculate, even if s/he happens to get things totally wrong. Don't worry if this creates a very incomplete or lopsided picture of things. Don't worry if Character A's view of events is partial or even entirely false. One-sidedness is part of the point here. You are only telling one side of the story.

Now tell the story a third time from the perspective of Character B. Keep the same third-person narrator you used for the previous version, but present the events through Character B's eyes. Again your possibilities will be restricted. But this time the restriction is likely to be even greater. You will be limited to the perceptions of a character who knows less than Character A. At least this is true of B's knowledge of A's secret. It is, of course, quite possible that about other things B knows more than A – about the consequences of A's actions, for example.

Focus 2

Your fourth version of the story should be from the perspective of Character C. Again, use the same third-person narrator to see the story through C's eyes. Does C know things that A and B don't? What does C get right and what does s/he get wrong? Is there a final right and wrong in the story, or is it all a matter of perspective?

Write the story one last time from the perspective of a complete outsider. Still use the same third-person narrator, but let him or her look through the eyes of an uninvolved bystander – perhaps some-one who just happens to see the whole thing from a bustop, or even from the top of a bus. This time there are bound to be a lot of gaps in understanding, and maybe even some pretty wayward attempts at interpretation. There is clearly a potential for comedy here, but also for a more disturbing twist to events if the outsider, having got things completely wrong, attempts to intervene…

What does this exercise show us? Above all it shows that the same story can sound very different when told from the point of view of different characters. If you have done all five versions carefully and consistently, you will probably have produced five quite different stories. You may also find that one version works much better than another. Perhaps one version creates fruitful suspense and ambi-guity, whereas another leaves too many questions unanswered.

This is a valuable exercise to come back to whenever you are writ-ing a piece of fiction. Even if you have already decided from whose point of view you want to tell your story, stop and experiment with a different perspective. There are three benefits to be gained from doing this. First, it will, at the very least, help you to know and understand your characters better. Even if you don't decide to use any of the alternative perspectives, they will have given you a fuller all-round understanding of the world of your story than you had before. Remember, the writer always needs to know a lot more about his or her characters – their backgrounds, their thoughts, their hopes and fears – than is ever finally communicated to the reader. Secondly, you may well find that an alternative perspective opens up possibilities you hadn't thought of, unexpected twists in the story. Again, this needn't involve adopting the new perspective – although there is no reason why it shouldn't. It could simply involve pursuing some of the narrative strands the new perspec-tive has suggested. Thirdly, experimenting with perspective will help you to think more objectively about your story. You need to be able to treat your writing as a sculptor might treat a lump of clay, shaping it first this way, then that. We all tend to get too attached to the way we do things. Any exercise that gets us into the habit of remembering that there are always alternatives can only do us good.

2. Style

Doing Voices

All people have different voices. Today, voices are often used as means of electronically testing identity. When friends call us on the phone, we usually know who they are just from the tone of their voice. But identity resides in more than just the grain or tone of the voice. It also has to with styles of speech – the types of vocabulary we use, the way we string our sentences together, the words we do or don't stress.

Your three characters will also have very different voices, voices you will have to get to know well in order to write about them. Look back over what you have written about them. Did the style of your writing change as you changed the perspectives you were writing from? In telling the story from the point of view of one character, you may want to bring the reader closer to him or her by trying to imitate the way the character would have told the story.

Exercise

Take each of your three characters in turn and get them to talk in their own voices. For each character, write three short monologues (they need only be about half a page). As themes for the monologues you might take something like: Home, A Funeral, Shopping. Choose themes of your own which will best bring out the character's voice. In this instance, how the character speaks is more important than what s/he says.

When you are satisfied that you have found your way into your character's voice, go back to the three versions of your story written from the perspective of each of your characters. Now rewrite all three in the voice of the character concerned. Don't write in the first person. That is, don't make the character the narrator. The narrator continues to write in the third person, but uses the speech style of the character from whose perspective the story is told.

Applications

Of course this is just an exercise. But it's a very useful one. Accompanying shifts of perspective with shifts of voice can be a very powerful way of sustaining a strong sense of character, without having to rely on any forms of explicit characterization. For a superb example of how effective this can be, have a look at NICK HORNBY'S *About a Boy*. Here not only the point of view, but also the narrative style, alternates with each chapter. You will find more complex, but equally effective, examples in the novels of HENRY JAMES. JAMES'S *The Wings of the Dove* is a masterpiece of ventriloquism. Look, for example, at how different the narrative voice is when parts of the story are told from the point of view of Merton Densher, Susan Shepherd, or even Aunt Maud.

Now we are going to do with voice the same thing we did with perspective. We shall retell the story five more times, using five different voices. The aim is both to practise writing in different styles, and to see how these different styles colour our reading of the story. The more effective the voices are, the more different your stories will become.

Think carefully about which perspective you will use for each of the five voices we are going to try. Ask yourself which point of view will work best with which voice.

We'll begin as simply as possible. The first voice speaks in very short, straightforward sentences.

It might be helpful to look at writers with a direct and simple style for inspiration. Try a short story by HEMINGWAY – "The Battler" for example. Or try the first few pages of ARUNDHATI ROY'S *The God of Small Things*, or A.L. KENNEDY'S short story "Animal".

Actually, the styles of writers like these are deceptively simple. It is harder to write good short sentences than one thinks. Notice how, even when writing short sentences, it remains important to vary word patterns and rhythms. If every sentence has more or less the same structure, your prose will very quickly become boring to the ear.

What effect does writing in shorter sentences have on your story? Do some parts work better than others? Which parts benefit and why? Of course this is just an exercise. Under most normal writing conditions you would vary sentence lengths. This exercise may help you to get a feel for what things are best kept short.

This time we're going to write long sentences. You can make the sentence structures as complicated as you like. That means plenty of subordinate clauses and parenthetical phrases and remarks. Try not, at this stage, to give in to the temptation to write parody or caricature. You may find that, to your ear, long sentences sound funny or old-fashioned. But keep your sentences serious; make sure they get across the information you want to convey clearly and effectively. All you will be doing is packing more information than usual into each unit. Again, remember to choose a suitable perspective from which to tell the story. Do you have a character whose style of thinking or whose way of looking at the world could conceivably be expressed in long, complex sentences? If not, you might want to tell the story from the point of view of an all-seeing, all-knowing narrator – as in the bird's-eye-view exercise in the perspective section of this chapter.

For help, you can turn to nearly any of the great novelists of the nineteenth century. They clearly made greater demands on the concentration of their readers than we seem to. Try, for example,

the second paragraph of GEORGE ELIOT's *Daniel Deronda* – it's just one sentence. On a lighter note, have a look at the description of the Circumlocution Office in Chapter 10 of DICKENS's *Little Dorrit*. This is DICKENS poking fun at convoluted speech and thought. But have a look at the first two paragraphs of the previous chapter of the novel. DICKENS himself can stretch a sentence in a perfectly clear and supple way.

A well-controlled long sentence can be a very powerful tool. It can evoke a remarkable sense of qualified detail, and reflect a mind for which such accuracy of perception and representation is important. Look at the opening pages of *The Ambassadors* by HENRY JAMES. Not all of the sentences are long, but even the shorter ones are packed with discriminating perceptions which tell us a great deal about how the character perceives the world.

In the first paragraph of *To the Lighthouse*, on the other hand, notice how VIRGINIA WOOLF creates an ironic distance from her character by describing the mind and thoughts of a six-year-old boy in language he would not be capable of using.

This is an interesting technique to try. If you want to present one of your characters ironically, write the story from his or her perspective but in sentences that s/he would never actually use.

Finally, for one quite extraordinary contemporary example of what a long sentence can do, take a look at W.G. SEBALD's last novel, *Austerlitz*. There is one sentence that spreads over ten pages – pp. 339–50 in the German edition (Fischer, 2003) and pp. 331–342 in ANTHEA BELL's English translation (Penguin, 2002).

Questions

What effect has the extension of sentences had on your story? It should feel like a very different piece of writing. Did you manage to keep the sentences lively and readable? Were you able to stop them sounding puffed up and ridiculous? Pick out the sentences that work least well and rewrite them. Sustaining long sentences and keeping them perfectly precise and understandable at the same time is an excellent discipline for a writer.

Imitation

This time, reformulate your story in the style of a writer you admire. This is more difficult than it may immediately appear. The first thing you have to do is get to understand how the style of your chosen writer works. Don't choose a writer merely because you like the things s/he writes *about*. Chose someone who says things in a *way* that particularly interests you.

Identifying how a style works demands that you become a highly sensitive literary critic. Writers naturally tend to make good close readers because they are just as fascinated by the "how" of craft as by the "what" of content. Today, a great many writers are also professional critics, book reviewers and teachers of literature.

The first thing to do is to find a passage by your chosen writer that really brings out the characteristic element of his or her style. Identify the effects the style achieves and how it goes about achieving them. What devices does it employ? Is it largely a question of rhythm? Or of the choice of words? Or of the order of the words?

While JAMES JOYCE was writing *Ulysses,* his friend FRANK BUDGEN once asked him how much he had written that day. Two sentences, replied JOYCE. Aha, said Budgen, you were looking for the right words. Oh no, said, JOYCE. I had the right words; I was looking for the right order to put them in. The two sentences were: *"Perfume of embraces all him assailed. With hungered flesh obscurely, he mutely craved to adore."*

Once you think you understand how the passage you have chosen works, try to write a passage of your own in exactly the same style. And I mean exactly. Use the same number of words per sentence. Reproduce the same rhythms, the same syntax, and the same rhetorical figures. Where your author uses a metaphor, you use one.

When you are happy that your paragraph sounds just as though it had been written by your chosen author, turn back to your own original story. Rewrite the entire piece in the style you have been working with.

Are there any places in your new version of the story that don't sound like your chosen author? Go on tinkering with them until they work.

Again, ask yourself how the new voice changes the whole feel of your story. Does the style work for the story? If the answer is: yes, in some places, but not in others, try to identify the places where it works and to figure out why it does.

Finally, take over the voice of a writer whose style you find worthy of parody or caricature. This can be a style you admire, but it can also be one you really don't like. The procedure is exactly the same as for the imitation exercise. First choose a characteristic passage, then write your own mirror image of it, and then rewrite your story in the same voice.

You will need to take a strong and recognizable style in order to produce a parody. The contours of the style have to be pretty clearly marked in the first place. If you are stuck for an example, try the introduction of Merton Densher in HENRY JAMES'S *The Wings of the Dove.* It is at the very beginning of Book 2, Chapter 3. Here, as a taster, is the beginning of the second paragraph:

He was young for the House of Commons, he was loose for the Army. He was refined, as may have been said, for the City and, quite apart from

the cut of his cloth, sceptical it might have been felt, for the Church. On the other hand he was credulous for diplomacy, or perhaps even for science, while he was perhaps at the same time too much in his mere senses for poetry and yet too little in them for art. You would have got fairly near him by making out in his eyes the potential recognition of ideas; but you would have quite fallen away again on the question of the ideas themselves. The difficulty with Densher was that he looked vague without looking weak – idle without looking empty.

You might also take a look at the beginning of LAURENCE STERNE'S *The Life and Opinions of Tristram Shandy*. This is a delightful style that is already very close to self-caricature.

Questions

You now have four stylistically different versions of your story. Each version should have shown you something new about the possibilities of different styles. The rhythms of one style may have been appropriate for some aspects of the story, but an absolute impediment or obstacle to expression in others. Read them through again, thinking about what works where.

Your Own Voice

Finally, you can drop all the shackles you have been imposing on yourself during the last exercise. This time, the aim is to put what you have learnt to good use. Write the story one more time in your own voice. This means you are completely free to vary sentence length, rhythm, register, idiom, rhetoric in the manner you find most appropriate to what you are saying.

3. Narrators and Narrative Distance

Note

If you are getting fed up with your story by now, put it away and come back to this exercise in a couple of days. If you can keep going, however, all well and good.

Preliminaries

In this section, we are going to do some thinking and writing about story-tellers and their relationship to the stories they tell. We have already looked at two types of third-person narrators: those who tell the story from above, and those who tell the story through the eyes of a particular character.

What other kinds of narrator are there, and how do they differ? How does the choice of a particular narrator affect the story narrated?

In this section we shall be concerned above all with first and second-person narrators, and with the question of narrative distance.

Aims

The aim of the section will be to produce three new versions of your story. One will be narrated in the first person singular (I), one in the second person singular (You). The third will be narrated by a third-person narrator who detests the main character in the story (and doesn't hide his or her feelings from the reader).

Before we get onto the writing, however, we need to do a bit of thinking about how our narrators stand in relation to the stories they narrate.

Distance

This is what is meant by *narrative distance* – the relationship between the story-teller and the story told. For the purposes of this section, narrative distance will be seen above all as a question of time and sympathy. How much time has passed between the moment in which the events of the story are supposed to have taken place and the time of its telling? Does the person telling the story sympathize with his or her characters, or does s/he write about them from an ironic or critical distance?

Another form of distance concerns the author's relation to his or her narrator. Do you want your narrator to come across as basically likeable or downright objectionable? Do you want to make it clear to the reader that your narrator's values and opinions are not your own – without stepping into the fray and *telling* the reader directly what you think? (An example of how to do this with a first-person narrator is given in Example 2 below).

One further aspect of narrative distance that will be useful to consider is the degree to which the narrator's presence can be perceived by the reader. In some stories, we are continually reminded of the presence of the story-teller (as commentator, explainer, judge), whereas in other stories we are made to forget entirely that they are narrated by anyone at all.

"I"

We can begin to unpack all these questions of person and distance by taking a look at some stories written in the first person.

Example 1

I did not know when I was a boy that most people in the world went away to school. I only knew that no one from my family had ever left the stilted farmhouse in the forest river, to travel thirteen miles in two days to arrive, with the mud dry on my bare feet, at the big white school where they laughed at the way my family had always spoken. (PHILIP HENSHER, "Dead Languages")

Example 2

I do not care for posturing women. But she struck me. I had to stop and look at her. The legs were well apart, the right foot boldly advanced, the left trailing with studied casualness. ... Very artificial the whole thing, but then I am not a simple man ... Sometimes as I hurried by (I am a man in a hurry) I allowed myself a quick glance and she seemed to beckon me, to welcome me out of the cold. Other days I remember seeing her in that tired, dejected passivity which fools mistake for femininity. (IAN MCEWAN "Dead as They Come")

Comment

Each example illustrates a different aspect of narrative distance. In Example 1, it is a distance in time. The narrator, now a man,

is writing about when he was still a boy. The "I" in the story is younger than the "I" telling it. Probably the most famous exploration of this temporal distance is CHARLES DICKENS'S *Great Expectations*.

In Example 2, it gradually becomes apparent that we are not meant to approve of the "I" who speaks in the story. This becomes increasingly clear as the story goes on. The narrator is looking at, then buys himself, then makes love to a dummy mannequin from a shop window. He ends up destroying her. In this case it is the author who is setting the narrator up. He gives him a rather arrogant voice and makes him say – increasingly – outrageous things.

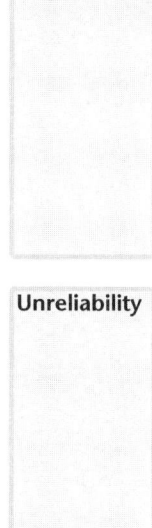

You can also create the same kind of distance from a third-person narrator. If the narrator's story is full of inconsistencies, the reader will question his or her reliability. If these inconsistencies are not just a product of a poorly thought-out plot, the effect can be powerful. Mistrusting the narrator's view of things, the reader is forced to put together his or her own version of events.

Unreliability

For a classic example of a first-person unreliable narrator see EDGAR ALAN POE's short story "The Tell-Tale Heart". For an example of third-person unreliable narration, see GRAHAM SWIFT's short story "Learning to Swim".

But let's stay with the first person a moment longer. Sometimes a third-person narrator will intrude into the story and offer a comment or an explanation, or a judgement in the first person.

Another "I"

Eighteenth century fiction is full of such intrusions, often couched in modes of address like "Dear Reader". In *Tom Jones*, HENRY FIELDING offers the following warning in the second chapter:

Reader, I think proper, before we proceed any farther together, to acquaint thee that I intend to digress, through this whole history, as often as I see occasion, of which I am myself a better judge than any pitiful critic whatever …

And FIELDING regularly interposes, usually in the first person, throughout the rest of the novel.

Notice that the use of the "I" in such intrusions is not the same as first-person narration as such. The intruding "I" is not a character in the story, whereas the first-person narrator is.

It is also worth remembering that the term "third-person narrator" is really no more than short-hand for a first-person narrator who narrates predominantly or exclusively in the third person. The first person is always in principle available to such a narrator, even if s/he never actually uses it in order to intrude into the narrative.

Intrusion	How intrusive do you want your narrator to be? In other words, to what degree should your reader be aware of the presence of a story-teller, shaping and formulating events? The more your narrator comments on or judges and interprets the story, the more perceptible s/he will be. Some narrators even get so involved as to tell the reader in advance what will or will not happen. ANTHONY TROLLOPE in *Barchester Towers* (1857) provides a famous example:

But let the gentle-hearted reader be under no apprehension whatsoever. It is not destined that Eleanor shall marry Mr. Slope or Bertie Stanhope.

Such intrusions are not necessarily fashionable, but there is absolutely no reason why they cannot still be effective or amusing in a piece of fiction. It would certainly be foolish to imagine that books like *Barchester Towers* or *Tristram Shandy* are any the worse for them. All we need to remember is that to use such devices now is inevitably to echo an older style of fiction. If such an echo is part of the desired effect, the device is fully justified.

Exercise	Experiment with different degrees of narratorial presence. Take just the first paragraph of your story and try telling it in the style of TROLLOPE or FIELDING or STERNE. Then try telling it in such a way that your reader will think you are either biased, or not telling the whole truth.

"You"	What happens when you tell a story in the second person singular?

Again, try rewriting the first paragraph of your story in the *you* form. Read what you've written. Who is this *you*?

Three Yous	It is likely that your *you* is one of three entities. Say you have chosen to write the story with Character B as your narrator. Character B is watching Character A, and writes about him or her in the second person. Of Character B, Character A says: You do this, you do that, you feel lonely, you feel deliriously happy, you find this funny, you find that absurd, etc. In this instance the "you" is a definable person, and the narrator is not just watching that person but getting inside his or her head.

But we also use "you" in other ways. We use "you", for example, to refer to a general non-specified person. In this case it is simply a slightly more colloquial version of "one": "you know how it is, when it's freezing cold in the morning and you really don't want to get out of bed" – that kind of thing.

Thirdly, "you" can also be a kind of "I". A second-person narrative often simply records a character talking to him- or herself. This kind of "self-communing" *you* can be very useful. It allows us to talk about ourselves under the thin disguise of talking about

CHAPTER 4   Telling a Story Again

someone else. Whether or not you decide to use this "self-com-muning" *you* in your story, do experiment with it in your note-books. Write about yourself in the second person and see if it frees up things you might not say if you were using "I".

For good examples of second-person narrative, look at Joyce Carol Oates's "You", or Samuel Beckett's "That Time". Beckett's *Company* is also very interesting for its negotiations between the second and third person. For a longer example of second person narrative, try Italo Calvino's *If on a winter night you meet a traveller.*

Examples

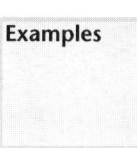

4. Order

You've probably heard it said a hundred times that a story needs a beginning, a middle, and an end. Aristotle said it, and people have been saying it ever since. More recently, the French film director, Jean-Luc Godard, offered an interesting proviso. A story, said Godard, needs a beginning, a middle, and an end – but not necessarily in that order. This is a very useful way of thinking about the ordering of information in a story.

Focus

We talked earlier about conceiving your story in three basic blocks: a wish, an accident, and a consequence. We marked one block with a square, another with a circle and the third with a triangle.

Blocks

Now take these three geometrical figures and write out all the different permutations they can produce: □ △ ○; □ △ ○; □ △ ○; □ △ ○, etc. There should be six in all.

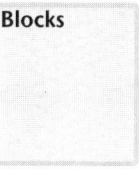

What will happen to your story if you write it out according to these six permutations of order? You probably won't want to reproduce your story another six times, but at least have a go at one or two variations, and work out the others in your head.

Experiment

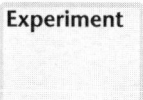

Playing with the basic order of events will almost inevitably pro-duce different types of story. Beginning at the end, for example, may give away the final punchline, but it can create a very dif-ferent, and sometimes equally compelling sense of suspense. Here the reader wants to know how a state of affairs came about.

Results

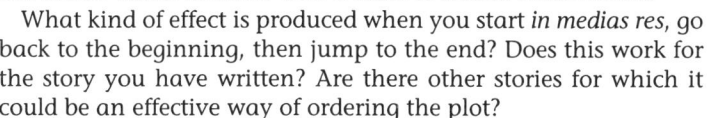

What kind of effect is produced when you start *in medias res*, go back to the beginning, then jump to the end? Does this work for the story you have written? Are there other stories for which it could be an effective way of ordering the plot?

You need to ask yourself these questions every time you write a story. They are equally important when working with longer forms, like the novel. Get into the habit of radically rejigging your plot – at least in your head or in your notebooks. The first order you come up with may not always be the best.

Conclusions

In this chapter we have been a bit like a boxer doing press-ups or a golfer practising various types of swing. We have been stretching our narrative muscles and lubricating our technical joints. If you've been very lucky, you may have ended up with one version of a story that you feel is worth working up into something finished and readable. But that hasn't been the point. What we've been doing is exploring the potential for doing things differently. We've not only been experimenting with techniques, but also training ourselves to get into good habits. I hope these habits will stick, and that you'll get used to bearing in mind all the possibilities we've been looking at whenever you write a story. And I hope you'll find the breadth of possible ways of telling a story liberating rather than daunting. Only you can know when you've finally got your story right. But at least you shouldn't be stuck for things to try when you feel it's still not quite there.

CHAPTER 5 Writing Poems: Breaking Lines

If your main interest as a writer is in writing poetry, you may well have leapt straight to this chapter and skipped the ones on prose fiction. I would strongly suggest, however, that you go back and read Chapters 1 and 2. They are all about exercising the imagination, generating ideas and tapping one's creative potential, and they are aimed at helping poets just as much as short-story writers.

Note for Poets

This chapter offers some first thoughts about writing poetry. It starts off with some fairly elementary questions about what poetry is and why we read and write it, then takes a brief look at how we can help our poems into existence. Finally, it starts putting its findings to work through a series of simple exercises.

Focus

1 What is a Poem?

What is a poem? This is ultimately an impossible question to answer. However, there is much to be learnt from looking at some of our more spontaneous responses.

Definitions

Poems are short, aren't they? Well, no, not necessarily. HOMER'S *Iliad* and WORDSWORTH'S *The Prelude* are both poems, but neither is short. There are long epic and narrative poems just as there are short lyrical ones.

Poems are about feelings. Some are, but not all. POPE'S *Essay on Criticism* is a highly intellectual meditation about the craft of writing, and there are countless philosophical investigations, theological ruminations and political protestations in verse.

Poems have to rhyme, or at least have a regular metre. Classical Greek poetry didn't rhyme. MILTON, who used rhyme to great effect in his shorter poems, didn't use it in *Paradise Lost*, referring to it in his note on "The Verse" as "the Invention of a barbarous Age, to set off wretched matter and lame Meeter". And at least since the beginning of the twentieth century thousands of poets have written in "free verse" without either regular metre or rhyme.

So what makes a poem a poem? Part of the answer has to be: the reader does. It is the way we read a text that defines it as poetry. We read poems differently from the way we read other texts. We pay special attention to things we might ignore when reading a novel or an article in the newspaper.

Attention

Mind the gap. If you have ever travelled on the London Underground you will have heard this expression. It is a warning announced over a loudspeaker when there is a space between the platform and an incoming train. Passengers are warned not to fall into the gap when getting on or off. I think we'd all agree that the phrase "Mind the gap" is not, in itself, a poem. But imagine you've just opened up an anthology of new London poetry and on page 29 you find this:

> *Mind*
> *the*
> *gap*

How do you respond? You probably don't look down at your feet to see if the ground has opened up beneath you. Instead, you probably begin asking yourself what these words mean *here*. If you have any experience of reading poems, you will know that every word demands a particular kind of attention. Take the first word, *mind.* It can mean "watch out" or "be careful", but it can mean plenty of other things, too. Think of it as a noun: the mind. You might already be beginning to hear the poem differently, with a little pause after the word *mind* – like this, perhaps: "Mind: the gap". But what does it mean to think of the mind as a gap? Is the mind an empty space in which everything gets lost? And what kind of gap? The gap between people, between self and world? The mind is the gap between ourselves and others; we imagine our own isolation. This isolation is corroborated by the three isolated monosyllables that make up the poem. They are semantically connected, but they stand alone in the open, empty space of the big page.

You may think this "over-interpretation" of the "poem" is absurd. The point, however, is that it catches us in the act, as it were, of reading poetry. We never think of all these things when we hear the phrase "Mind the gap" on the underground. But as soon as we imagine we are reading a poem, we start to read differently. We look out for ambiguities, we pay attention to details of shape and form – we start minding the gaps.

Poems become poems when they are read as poems. Poetry is, at least in part, a matter of the attention we pay to a text, as well as of the properties that belong to the text itself. This attention is triggered above all by the context in which we are reading. Three words looked at in a poetry anthology or poetry seminar will start meaning something very different from what they might mean in any other context.

But is this really enough for a definition of poetry? Aren't we missing something?

Yes, we are missing something. But this something isn't deep feelings, intellectual honesty, or highly crafted use of language – although all of these things *can* be constituents of good poetry. What we are missing are line breaks. One of the things that made us read "Mind the gap" as a poem was that the phrase had been broken into free-standing lines. This is an earth-shattering truth – the closest we can come to a definition of poetry that really works. Poems are written in lines. Where the lines begin and end is a matter of great importance. Look at where the lines end on any page of a novel. Would anything be drastically altered if you slightly narrowed or widened the page and the first line ended on "the" instead of "door" and the second line ended on "impertinently" instead of "and"? Presumably not. Now take a sonnet by SHAKESPEARE and change the line endings:

Shall I compare thee to
A summer's day? Thou art more lovely and more temperate:
rough winds do
Shake the darling buds of
May, but summer's lease hath
All too short a date.

Something has clearly gone wrong here. In this case it is primarily a question of sound. The lines have to end where they do because of the rhyme. But rhyme is only one of many criteria on the basis of which poets choose to break their lines. We'll be looking at some others later in this chapter.

Let's have another go at a working definition of poetry. By this I mean above all a definition that will work for us as writers of poems. A poem is a piece of writing to which the reader decides to pay a particular kind of attention to meaning, shape and form. This decision is triggered both by the context in which the reader encounters the text, and by the reader's impression that where the lines begin and end is a matter of great importance.

Why have we spent so much time on thinking about what poetry is and is not? Because the conclusions we have reached will remain among the most important lessons we have to learn about writing poetry. Whatever we write will have to do two very basic things. It will have to reward the close attention it will demand by being written in lines, and the breaks between the lines – as the very features that define our texts as poems – will have to be full of purpose.

2 Why do we read poems, and why do we write them?

Readability
So far we have only talked about what poetry, reduced to its bare essentials, actually is. The very worst doggerel will satisfy the basic requirements of our definition. What is it, then, that makes some poems readable, others even publishable, and others still instantly forgettable? And how does one go about producing the first kind and avoiding the third?

It is one thing to write poems just for oneself, and another to hope to be read with pleasure by others. Many people write for their own entertainment or solace, and there is nothing wrong with writing poems for therapeutic reasons. In these two chapters on poetry, however, I will be assuming that you want your poetry to be read – in which case very different criteria of workmanship and judgement apply.

Ingredients
What kind of ingredients does your poetry have to have in order to be readable for others? Obviously, opinions will differ on what constitutes a good poem, but there are three basic ingredients that most readers and writers of poetry would recognize as absolutely essential.

Freshness
All good poetry gives us what Robert Frost called "a fresh look and a fresh listen." It enables us both to see our world differently and to hear new potential in the language we use. Good poetry surprises us, and the better it is, the longer it goes on doing so. Read SHAKESPEARE'S Sonnet 73 and take a close look at the final couplet:

This thou perceiv'st, which makes thy love more strong,
To love that well, which thou must leave ere long.

Does the word "that" in the last line refer to the beloved or to life itself? The recognition that it refers to both still comes as a surprise, a shock even, and this poem was written nearly five hundred years ago.

Memorable Speech
W.H. AUDEN called poetry "memorable speech". People who like poetry in the first place tend to be able to quote it from memory. This is because the language of a good poem really sits; one feels it couldn't have been put any other way. The words offer a unique insight into the things being evoked, the sound fits the sense, and there is a living tension between parts and whole. This does not mean that the language has to be especially elaborate or difficult or odd. The simplest poems can often be the most memorable, although there often is, to be sure, something deceptive about their simplicity. Take, for example, PHILIP LARKIN'S "Talking in Bed", first published in 1960:

Talking in bed ought to be easiest,
Lying there together goes back so far,
An emblem of two people being honest.

Yet more and more time passes silently.
Outside, the wind's incomplete unrest
Builds and disperses clouds about the sky,

And dark towns heap up on the horizon.
None of this cares for us. Nothing shows why
At this unique distance from isolation

It becomes still more difficult to find
Words at once true and kind,
Or not untrue and not unkind.

Almost every line of this poem remains fresh and memorable. The double meaning of "lying" in the second line still surprises, as does the conceit in line 9. The literal meaning of "this unique distance from isolation" is closeness, companionship, union, but the words themselves suggest the very opposite. The rhyme scheme of the poem is surprising, too – that is, the realization that it actually does rhyme very carefully all the way through. In addition to the gentle near-rhymes of "easiest" and "honest", "horizon" and "isolation", and the suggested eye-rhyme of "silently" and "sky", there are the rhymes between the last line of one stanza and the middle line of the next: "honest" / "unrest", "sky" / "why". The poem lodges itself in the memory before one really knows why. It is a characteristically Larkinesque example of the art that conceals art.

Perhaps most memorable of all, however, are the last two lines. The double negation of "not untrue and not unkind" hits very hard. The difference that it registers (from "true and kind") is the very stuff of poetry – an eye for the finer shades of difference between things, and between the words that strive to express them.

Authenticity

Every poet imitates other poets and there is no great poetry without influence. But imitation and influence are not in themselves what makes a poem good. The essence of the poem has to be fundamentally your own; it is something – however small or inconsequential – that you and only you have seen, felt and expressed in that particular form. It is precisely the uniqueness of your experience of the world, your way of making sense of experience and your way of expressing it in words that will make your writing of interest to others. But you have to learn to experience the world keenly, to reflect on that experience honestly, and to articulate it truly – so that what comes out really is you, and not some received view of things.

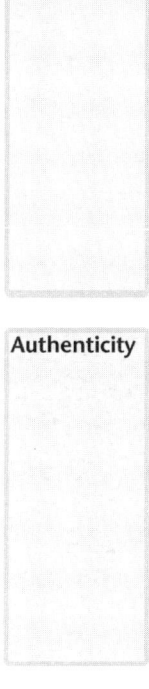

This doesn't mean that you have to have personally experienced all the things you write about. You can write about a journey to Saturn, about being the lace in a shoe, or a cat stuck up a tree. But the imaginative experience still has to be true.

Poetry and the World

Great poetry is timeless, but it is none the less a product of and a response to its own time. All serious writing involves a serious engagement with the world, and not a retreat from it into the bastions of the inner self. The view of the poet as a recluse, anxiously protecting his or her sacred word-horde from all contaminating contact with real life is a very unhelpful fiction. SIR PHILIP SIDNEY was a highly active courtier, governor and soldier, and WALLACE STEVENS – one of the most profoundly philosophical poets of the twentieth century – worked for the Hartford Accident and Indemnity Company from 1916 until his death in 1955. Like all writers, poets are in touch with contemporary reality; they read the newspapers, and keep their fingers on the pulse of the language of their time.

Poetry and the Present

You, your language, and your poetry are inevitably shaped by the time in which you live. It is true that we often start to write because we are in love with the poetry of someone else. But this is only a means towards finding a voice of our own. Beginning writers will often ask: "Why shouldn't I write like WORDSWORTH, his poetry is wonderful." WORDSWORTH'S poetry is wonderful, but – for better or worse – he wouldn't have written it had he been writing at the beginning of the twentieth century. WORDSWORTH'S language of "men speaking to men" was a reaction against what he saw as the stilted diction of the neo-classical poetry of the eighteenth century. We do not have to react against that sort of diction today; we have other types of speech to react to. WORDSWORTH had to write the way he did in order to respond to his world as he experienced it. We have to find a language that responds to our world, not WORDSWORTH'S.

Again, it is all a matter of freshness, memorable speech, and authenticity. The language of good poetry is often memorable precisely because it is fresh – because it differs from a way of saying things that we have grown used to. And it is authentic because it says things the way they have to be said now, and not the way someone else said them, responding to a very different set of circumstances in a very different time.

Reading

For this very reason, it is absolutely essential that poets be deeply familiar with the poetry of their own time. Just as WORDSWORTH was responding to his own age and to the poetry that led up to it, so our poets continue to find new ways of formulating new (and old) experiences and of responding to the formulations of others. You don't have to like everything you read. It is fine to be inspired by negative examples to write something new. But make sure you know where poetry has been going over the last fifty years before you prematurely congratulate yourself on your own originality. If you find *all* contemporary poetry ugly, inconsequential, or "un-poetic", you are certainly missing something, and it is pretty unlikely that you will write readable poetry yourself.

③ Finding your poem

Resources

Most of our poems, like most of our stories, come from things we've seen and heard. We get our ideas by tapping imaginative resources that are already there. We looked at ways of uncovering and making use of these resources in Chapters 1 and 2. The sections on "Generating Ideas" and "Training the Senses" in Chapter 1, and the sections on "Finding Our Stories" and "Story Resources" in Chapter 2 will be, I hope, fundamentally relevant to poets. I shall assume here that you have read these sections and have tried out some of the exercises in them. All I want to add here are a few points of emphasis and focus that are, I think, particularly perti-nent to the writing of poetry.

Density

Poems, as we have already said, can be very long, but most of the focus in this book will be on shorter forms. More people write short poems than long ones, and if you are just starting out, you should in any case leave your great epic until you have got the hang of some shorter forms.

Precisely because they are short and the objects of intense critical attention, short poems tend to be fairly dense things. By dense I do not necessarily mean heavy, and I certainly don't mean unwieldy. I simply mean that there is not a lot of fat around the meat, or bubbles between the chocolate. Because there isn't a single word that could be removed without damaging the whole thing, each and every word carries an enormous burden of responsibility.

For this reason, a poet's attention to, and interest in, individual words tends to be even more intense than that of the writer of fic-tion. This inevitably affects the way poets work.

Notebooks 1

When writers of prose fiction overhear a snippet of conversation, they might get ideas about character or plot. Poets may get simi-lar ideas, but they will also take a special interest in the words themselves.

Poets' notebooks, then, will often contain scribblings about indi-vidual words – how they sound, how they look on the page, how their meaning changes when the second syllable is stressed, how odd they sound coming from the mouth of a civil servant, a milk-man, a child. Poets are, by definition, word fetishists; they want

to know all they can about words, their different meanings, sounds, spellings, histories.

Write down words that interest you – things you overhear, see on signposts, come across in your daily reading. Find out their histories, how their meanings have changed over time.

Notebooks 2   Something else you will often find in a poet's notebook are metrical patterns without words. Sometimes what comes to mind before the words of a poem – even before the basic idea – is simply a rhythm. Rhythms can go on to suggest words, and moods, and ideas. If you get one in your head, jot it down; it might turn out to be very precious indeed. We'll look more closely at metre and rhythm (and how to transcribe them) in Chapter 6.

Ears   All writers have to train their senses, just as dancers train their limbs, but poets have a particularly sensuous relationship to words. Good poetry is nearly always first and foremost for the ear. Poets have to develop a heightened sensitivity to the relation between the sound of things and the sounds of words – and to the way words sound together. Get into the habit of reading poetry aloud. Reserve five minutes of every day to listen to the music of a poem as you read it aloud, allowing your tongue and palate to luxuriate in the shapes and sounds they produce. Always read your own poetry aloud; try to hear each line into being, and use your ears to correct unwanted awkwardnesses on the page.

Try listening to sounds you hear outside in the world around you. Try imitating them, using real or nonsense words. Write the words into your notebook with the name of the sound beside them.

Eyes   Poets also have a sensuous relationship to the physical appearance of words. Poems are for the eye as well as the ear. Some things you can only see and not hear, such as "eye-rhymes" like *come* and *home*, or *through* and *cough*. Prose writers don't have to think too much about the appearance of words on the page; poets do. Line breaks, as we shall see, can appeal to the eye as well as the ear. And some words simply look fascinating, out of place, disturbing, beautiful when put next to, or separated from, others. JOHN KINSELLA chose the title *Syzygy* for one of his collections: I bet he was drawn to the look of the word, as well as to its meaning.

Automatic Writing   Take another look at the automatic writing exercise in the third section of Chapter 1 (Generating Ideas). Try doing an exercise like this every day for two weeks. Don't re-read what you have written, but keep it in your notebook. When the two weeks are up, look through what you've done. Be on the lookout for surprising images, rhythms, collocations of words. There is almost bound to be at least one expression that fires your imagination. You may find an image that suggests a whole poem, or a striking title for a poem.

Write out the expressions you find most memorable onto a separate page in your notebook, so that you know where to find them when you need them.

❹ Line Breaks

We have said that where lines begin and where they end is a defining feature of poetry. I'd like to end this preliminary chapter on writing poetry with some thinking about how and why poets break lines in the places they do.

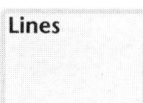

Lines

A good way to start thinking about line breaks is to take a piece of prose and chop it up into shorter lines. Anything will do: a newspaper article, a sentence or two from a novel. Try working with the same piece several times, each time putting in line breaks at different places. What differences do you see? Which versions work best, and why?

Breaking Prose

Here is the opening sentence of FLANNERY O'CONNOR'S short story "The Turkey": "His guns glinted sun steel in the ribs of the tree and, half aloud through a crack in his mouth, he growled, 'All right, Mason, this is as far as you go.'" And here are just two (out of hundreds of possible) ways of line-breaking the sentence. For added flexibility, I've dropped the first two commas.

Example

1).
His guns
glinted sun
steel
in the ribs
of the tree
and half aloud
through a crack
in his mouth
he growled,
'All right, Mason,
this is as far as you go.'

2).
His guns glinted sun
steel in the ribs
of the tree and half
aloud through a crack
in his mouth he growled,
'All right, Mason,
this is as far as you go.'

O'CONNOR'S sentence has undergone some fundamental changes. What strikes us first is the effect it now has on the ear. The first version "discovers" the rhyme in "guns" and "sun", and the near-rhymes "aloud", "mouth" and "growled". It also brings out some interesting rhythmic patterns. Notice how the lines "glinted SUN", "in the RIBS", "of the TREE", "through a CRACK" and "in his MOUTH" all have the same stress pattern. They are all anapaests: two unstressed syllables followed by a stressed one (although it is equally possible to read the first as "GLINTed SUN"). We shall look more closely at questions of rhythm and metre in Chapter 6; the point here is simply to show how line-breaking can bring out the rhythmic potential of words. Few readers would have noticed that the opening sentence of O'CONNOR'S story contains five anapaests – or at least four and a half if we chose to read the first as "GLINTed SUN".

The second version seems to go for a more regular stress pattern. Each line (except the last) has two stressed syllables:

His GUNS glinted SUN
STEEL in the RIBS
of the TREE and HALF
aLOUD through a CRACK
in his MOUTH he GROWLED,
'ALL right, MAson,
THIS is as FAR as you GO.

Both versions felt inclined to keep the last line as a single unit. The rhythm here seems to support the sense. The line is made up of three rhythmical units. "THIS is as", "FAR as you", and "Go". The first two units are dactyls – that is one stressed syllable followed by two unstressed one. The give a sense of movement to the line. The third unit is a thump: a single stressed syllable. It suggests that the movement has come to an end. And this, after all, is the sense of the line. FLANNERY O'CONNOR certainly knew this herself – even if she only knew it in her ear and not in her head. She won't have been thinking in terms of dactyls and anapaests, but – like all good prose writers – she was making use of a highly trained sense of rhythm.

The line breaks we have been looking at are above all for the ear. They let us hear something – such as rhyme and rhythmic pattern – that we would not otherwise have heard. This is one of the most important functions of line-breaking in poetry. But is it is not the only one.

Line breaks can also appeal to the eye and the mind. Take the first line-break in WALLACE STEVENS's "Man Carrying Thing":

The poem must resist the intelligence
Almost successfully...

The first line on its own means something different from the two lines taken together. We get two meanings for the price of one. When we grasp the second, we do not entirely forget the first. It goes on haunting what we read. This is precisely the point STEVENS is making: The poem must resist the intelligence / Almost successfully.... It both does and doesn't at the same time.

Another telling example of a line break which radically affects the meaning of the broken phrase is the opening of GEOFFREY HILL'S "September Song":

Undesirable you may have been, untouchable
you were not...

When the eye gets to the end of the first line, it reads untouchable in the same way as it had read undesirable: "You may have been undesirable and you may have been untouchable". The continuation of the phrase in the second line comes as a shock. It completely contradicts our initial reading. Now we understand: "You may have been undesirable, but you were *not* untouchable." Read the whole poem to see what is going on here. There are many other inspired line breaks.

Take a look at this odd sentence. "So much depends upon a red wheelbarrow glazed with rain water beside the white chickens." It is actually a poem by WILLIAM CARLOS WILLIAMS, with the line breaks taken out. When you put WILLIAMS'S line breaks back in, it looks like this:

Experiment

So much depends
upon

a red wheel
barrow

glazed with rain
water

beside the white
chickens.

As soon as we see it set out on the page like this, we know it's a poem. We might still be unsure of what it is trying to do, but there are several things about the line breaks that tell us it is doing something very conscious. In each verse (or stanza) there are four words: three in the first line and one in the second. There is also a pattern to the syllables: 4:2 in the first verse, 3:2 in the second, 3:2 in the third, and 4:2 again in the fourth. As soon as we recognize patterns like these, we know that they are not accidental –

Pattern

they haven't simply fallen from the sky. Someone has created these patterns for a reason. That's why we start to pay the words that special attention we afford to poetry. And the words pay us back handsomely.

Sense

There is much for the ear in this poem: the repetition of "r"s and "w"s, of "eɪ" sounds in "glazed with rain" and "aɪ" sounds in "Beside the white". But the line breaks are first and foremost for the mind's eye. Take, for example, the most radical one: "red wheel / barrow". At first we read "red wheel" then have our assumption challenged by "barrow" in the next line. "Barrow" comes as a surprise. Because of the simple line break, it remains fresh every time one looks at the poem.

Surprise

The whole poem is built around this principle of surprise. After "So much depends / Upon" one expects something grand, like love, or fortune, or hard work. But a red wheelbarrow? For whom can so much depend on that? Asking oneself who could speak these lines is a good way into the poem. Whenever I've looked at the poem in seminars, students have tended to come up with three answers. The first is: a farmer. But can you really imagine a farmer saying: "Well, son, so much depends upon a red wheelbarrow"? Isn't he more likely to say: so much depends upon the harvest or the price of barley. The second and third answers are that it could be a child or a painter. I find the combination of the two very revealing. PICASSO was once asked why his paintings looked so childish in their technique. He replied that he had been striving all his life to paint like a child. What he meant was that he wanted to represent the world with a fresh eye. This was what WILLIAM CARLOS WILLIAMS wanted, too. (The poem was written at the time PICASSO was moving beyond analytical cubism towards a more "naive" neo-classicism.) WILLIAMS (like WORDSWORTH two centuries before him) was fed up with what he saw as the inflated poetic rhetoric of previous generations, and strove for a fresh and objective look at things. What matters in art, the poem seems to tell us, is composition – putting one thing next to another – not high-sounding themes and overdressed expression. The poem came as a shock in the 1920s, and it still manages to surprise us now.

Exercise

I'd like to close this chapter with an exercise that will get us to put into practice some of the preaching I've been doing so far. An exercise, that is, on line-breaking and surprise. This exercise is best done in a workshop, or at least in a group of three. It can, if necessary, also be done alone, but at a cost to at least part of the surprise element.

Step 1

Write down the name of an animal with one (slightly silly) adjective to describe it. For example: an amorous armadillo, a poker-faced lemming or a homesick hyena. Then write down a somewhat bizarre activity, such as popping the bubbles in a glass of coke, or digging a hole with a teaspoon. Pass your animal to the person on your left, and the activity to the person on your right. (If you are doing the exercise alone, you will have to work with your own animal and activity).

Step 2

Now combine the animal and activity you have been given to make the first part of a simile. That is: "Like X (the animal you have been given) doing Y (the activity you have been given, ...)" Now invent the second part of the simile that (more or less) makes sense of the first. Do this by adding a clause that begins with he, she, I, or you. For example: Like a star-struck rattle-snake tipping the barber an Irish sixpence, he slipped through the door with a flick of his tongue. I'm sure you'll manage something better than that, but whatever you come up with – especially if you are working with others – it is bound to be a simile that has never been used before.

Step 3

Now that you have your totally original simile, try line-breaking it into a very short poem. Do several different versions, going for both ear-breaks and eye-breaks. Just for the fun of it, it's worth experimenting with going along the line trying out a new break after each word. Consider the differences in anticipated meaning triggered by doing this with the example above (being pretty free with the hyphens):

Like a star
struck rattle-snake;

or

Like a star-struck rattle
snake;

or

Like a star
struck rattle
snake tipping
the barber
an Irish
sixpence
he slipped
through the door
with a flick
of his tongue.

This is not a good poem, for sure; but it does begin to explore some of the techniques and strategies that might yet go into the writing of a better one.

6

CHAPTER Writing Poems: Sound and Sense

Art, not Chance

As Matthew Sweeney and John Hartley Williams remind us in *Writing Poetry* – one of the best books around on the subject – poetry is ten per cent inspiration and ninety per cent perspiration. This is not to say that poets never scribble down whole and very nearly finished poems in a mad, feverish rush. Occasionally they do – but even then it is only because of the hours, days, weeks, months, years of perspiration they have put into their work before this rare and fleeting moment arrives. Because every detail in a poem counts for so much, the making of a poem calls for considerable technical skill and craft, together with considerable intellectual discipline. The skill and craft can be learnt; the discipline can be practised. The more time and effort you put into these things, the better your poems will become.

Here are some lines from Alexander Pope's *An Essay on Criticism* (1711) about the art of making sense of sound in poetry. They are clearly the work of a great craftsman. We do not have to want to write like Pope, or even to like the way he writes, to recognize his craftsmanship.

True ease in writing comes from Art, not Chance,
As those move easiest who have learn'd to dance.
'Tis not enough no harshness gives offence;
The sound must seem an echo to the sense.
Soft is the strain when Zephyr gently blows,
And the smooth stream in smoother numbers flows:
But when loud surges lash the sounding shore,
The hoarse rough verse should like the torrent roar.

Focus

This chapter takes a very practical, writing-oriented look at sound and sense in poetry. It focuses on a number of basic issues, such as rhythm, metre and rhyme, alliteration and assonance. The point throughout is to start training the ear, not merely to develop an awareness of poetic devices for their own sake. Even if you never intend to write in a fixed form, involving regular metre and rhyme, you must be able to use these bread-and-butter devices. Free verse, as T.S. Eliot once suggested, is always *freed* verse; it is not a disregard for fixed form, but a response to it. Just as Picasso didn't paint distorted human figures because he couldn't paint "realistic" ones, any self-respecting poet will want to be able to use the formal devices he or she consciously chooses to do without.

1 Rhythm

There is no poetry without rhythm. The word *rhythm* comes from the Greek word *rhuthmos*: a measured movement, derived from *rhein*: to flow. Rhythm is a very broad concept. We talk about the rhythm of the seasons, the rhythm of the tide, of the body, of breathing, of the heart. Our days tend to have a rhythm, and we often get upset when that rhythm is broken. All these examples have at least two things in common: they all involve a kind of flow (*rheo*), and consist of patterns – that is, elements that can be repeated, even if only in changing, irregular forms.

Language is fundamentally rhythmical. All language, not just poetry and song. Our everyday speech necessarily involves flow and repetition. Otherwise we couldn't understand one another. Furthermore, we use rhythm in everyday speech to support the sense of what we are saying. "GET OUT!" is rhymthically more communicative than "Would you be so kind as to leave", although the latter can be strengthened rhythmically by adding an extra syllable: "Would you PLEASE be so KIND as to LEAVE". The effect of this last example is reminiscent of FLANNERY O'CONNOR'S similarly insistent phrase, "THIS is as FAR as you GO", discussed in the previous chapter.

Get into the habit of listening to the rhythms of everyday speech. How do people alter sound patterns to affect sense? Are there patterns that tend to suggest a certain sense in themselves, irrespective of the words they carry? What are the expressive properties of different rhythmic patterns, what can they do?

Write these rhythmic patterns down. There are several easy ways of doing this. You can mark stressed syllables with capital letters, as I have been doing here. But you should also get used to writing down rhythmic patterns without using words. The most conventional markers of stressed and unstressed syllables in the analysis of poetry are the symbols: "/" for a stressed syllable, and "v" for an unstressed one. The stress pattern of FLANNERY O'CONNOR'S "THIS is as FAR as you GO" would be written out as: / v v / v v /.

2 Metre

Metre is not quite the same as rhythm. It's more like regularized rhythm, a sustained and repeated rhythmic pattern, the continuation of which can readily be anticipated.

Definition

Feet	The basic units of metre are called feet. A foot is a combination of stressed and unstressed syllables. The most common feet in English poetry are:

the *iamb* – one unstressed syllable followed by a stressed one: v / (as in *enjoy*).

the *trochee* – one stressed syllable followed by an unstressed one: / v (as in *paper*).

the *anapaest* – two unstressed syllables followed by a stressed one: v v / (as in *interrupt*).

and the *dactyl* – one stressed syllable followed by two unstressed ones: / v v (as in *suddenly*).

Four other feet you should be aware of are:

the *spondee* – two consecutive stressed syllables: / / (as in *rough verse* in the eighth line of the excerpt from POPE's *An Essay on Criticism*).

the *pyrrhic* foot – two consecutive unstressed syllables: v v (often formed by clusters of prepositions, pronouns and articles like *in a* or *of her*, and often, in English verse, read as a component part of another foot like an anapaest or dactyl).

the *amphibrach* – one unstressed syllable followed by a stressed and then another unstressed syllable: v / v (as in *banana*).

and the *amphimacer* or *Cretic foot* – one stressed syllable followed by an unstressed and then another stressed syllable: / v / (as in *live your life*).

Lines of Feet	Lines are defined metrically by the number and types of feet they are made up of. A line with three feet is called a trimeter, one with four feet a tetrameter, with five feet a pentameter, and with six feet a hexameter – to name only the most common. If all the five feet of a pentameter are iambs, we speak of *iambic pentameter*, if all four feet of a tetrameter are trochees we call it *trochaic tetrameter*, and so on. The analysis of the metrical patterns of poetry is called *scansion*. We speak of *scanning* poems to work out their metre.

The properties of the individual feet directly affect the lines they appear in. The more unstressed syllables there are, the quicker the line will sound; the more stressed syllables, the slower.

Spondees are great line-slowers. Consider the end of the second line of KEATS's "Ode on a Grecian Urn":

Thou STILL unRAvished BRIDE of QUIetNESS,
Thou FOSTer-CHILD of SIlence and SLOW TIME

Both the syllables "slow" and "time" are stressed, which makes us slow down slightly as we speak them. This, of course, is "an echo to the sense" of the words themselves.

Anapaests, on the other hand, tend to create an impression of tripping swiftness, as illustrated by COLERIDGE in his *Metrical Feet:*

"With a LEAP and a BOUND the swift ANapaests THRONG" (v v / v v / v v / v v /).

Iambic pentameter is by far the most common metre in English poetry. This is probably because it comes close to the natural rhythms of ordinary English speech. It is not hard to speak without artifice in iambic pentameter: The OTHer DAY I MET a FRIEND of MINE / who'd SPENT his SUmmer HOliDAYS in SPAIN / and SAID he'd DONE a LOT of FISHing THERE, etc. Some novelists actually find themselves taking the strings of iambs out of their prose to stop it getting too monotonous. "To stop it getting too monotonous" is, by the way, also iambic pentameter!

An entirely predictable metre can be equally as monotonous in poetry. Most of SHAKESPEARE'S plays are written in *blank verse* (unrhymed iambic pentameter), but Shakespeare frequently varies the line. Consider his most famous line: "To be or not to be, that is the question". There are certainly five pulse-like stresses in the line, but they don't all fall in the "right" place for iambic pentameter. And there is also one syllable too many. One expects: v / v / v / v / v /, but because the word "that" is naturally stressed, what one gets is: v / v / v / / v v / v.

PHILIP LARKIN was also a master of building a flexible rhythmic pattern around a basic iambic pentameter form. Have another look at "Talking in Bed". All the lines in the first three stanzas have between nine and eleven syllables, and most of them have ten; they also have a clear five-beat pulse. Yet none of the lines is an unequivocal iambic pentameter. Lines one and two begin with trochees ("Talking", "Lying"). This is a handy way of deregularizing iambic pentameter. Also try scanning LARKIN'S "Home is so Sad", quoted below in the section on rhyme. It is another fine example of flexible variations on a basic pentameter line.

If you are using iambic pentameter and feel your lines are sounding a bit too "ti-tum ti-tum ti-tum ti-tum ti-tum", try beginning a line or two with a trochee, or adding an extra unstressed syllable somewhere to make an anapaest.

Metre is not an end in itself. Like every other part of the poem, it has to mean something and has to serve the poem as a whole. In his poem "The Voice", THOMAS HARDY writes about being haunted by the memory of his dead wife. His repeated use of dactyls (/ v v) supports this idea by creating an echo effect. This is already clear from the first line: "Woman much missed how you call to me, call to me" (/ v v / v v / v v / v v).

SHAKESPEARE wrote the whole of Sonnet 20 with *feminine endings* (that is lines which end on an unstressed rather than a stressed syllable). It is the only sonnet of his in which he did this in every line. Read Sonnet 20 and you'll see why he did this.

Take another look at the excerpt from ALEXANDER POPE's *An Essay on Criticism*. Try to scan each line and see how each metrical set-up supports the meaning it is intended to carry.

Pulsating Pentameters

It's high time we did a bit of writing, so I'm going to end this section on metre with a series of exercises. The focus will be on writing in iambic pentameter. Whether you will ultimately want to write poems in iambic pentameter is irrelevant here. The metre is so basic and intrinsic to English poetry that you have to be able to master it before going on to any other form. It's a bit like mastering the elementary scales if you're taking up the piano, or learning to breathe properly if you're starting to sing.

Exercise 1

I gave an example above of how easily ordinary speech can fall into iambic pentameter. Try saying out loud as many ordinary sentences as you can while keeping to the iambic pentameter pattern. Start with something like: "It's funny how the sweet-shop's always shut", or "I wonder if all poets play these games". Every time you get stuck or make a mistake, first solve the problem, then go back to the beginning and start again. Don't worry if what comes out is complete and utter nonsense. It's the flow (*rheo*) that we're interested in here, not the sense. Once the lines do start flowing and you really feel you've got the hang of it, you can begin writing your lines down. Try to scribble as many pages of iambic pentameter as possible, and as fast as you can. First try to fill a page, then two or three pages.

Exercise 2

Now that you have got the feel of the basic iambic pentameter pulse, we can start experimenting with different word-lengths. First write two lines of iambic pentameter using words of only one syllable. For example: "I'd like to know how long I'll have to wait. I've been here for the best part of an hour."

When you've done this, try writing two lines of iambic pentameter which contain at least five words with two syllables each. ("The only way I'm ever getting out" etc.)

Your next two lines should contain at least five trisyllabic words ("I have no memory of Christopher" etc.

Finally, try two lines of iambic pentameter using at least five words with four syllables ("The undertaker's discontented wife" etc).

Reflections

Which of these pairs of lines was most difficult to write? Which pair works best? Why? How has using words of different length affected your basic pentameter line? You will probably have found that using longer words, although difficult at first, adds an unexpected naturalness to the line. Lines like "A few cathedrals chronically on show" or "A shape less recognisable each week" (both from PHILIP LARKIN's "Church Going") sound a lot less staccato than "What can we do if all our words are short?". Both, of course, have

CHAPTER  Writing Poems: Sound and Sense

their place in a poem. The art is working out what is the right place.

Write the following line into your notebook: "The red bird flies across the golden floor". It's from a poem by WALLACE STEVENS, and we are going to use it as a starting point for three minutes of automatic writing. Don't write lines of poetry, and don't think about metre for the moment. Write continuous prose. Once you've started, don't lift your pen from the paper and don't stop to think. Use the line given as a point of departure and let your imagination race away with it.

Exercise 3

When the three minutes are up, look over what you have written. Try to find a phrase or sentence that forms an iambic pentameter. If you can't find one, take another that is nearly iambic pentameter, and adjust it. For example, you could change "the green mushrooms are in bloom" to "the green and mouldy mushrooms are in bloom".

Take STEVENS'S iambic pentameter line as the first line for a six-line poem. Make sure all the lines have five feet – that is, five clearly stressed syllables – but feel free to vary the feet. Start some lines with a trochee; add an anapaest or a dactyl whenever one suggests itself. Try your best *not* to use any rhymes.

Take this line as your starter: "My mother is an alien, her hands...". Go on from there, writing whatever comes into your head, but keeping strictly to the iambic pentameter pattern. Again, try not to rhyme. Write fourteen lines.

Exercise 5

Do practise these exercises regularly at first. The aim is to develop a feel for the pulse of a line. If you can do it with iambic pentameter, you'll be able to do it with other (including more irregular) forms. Think of these exercises as daily warm-ups. They will not only improve your sense of rhythm, but will also free up your unconscious. They'll help you build up a store of lines and images that will come in very handy later.

Practice

You can always return to these exercises when you are stuck for ideas. Automatic writing has a habit of telling you what it is you didn't even know you wanted to write about. You can also trawl through the results of your earlier exercises for flashes of inspiration.

3 Rhyme

In Exercises 4 and 5 above, I suggested that you avoid using rhyme. Rhyme should, at all times, be used with caution. It is very easy to rhyme badly and immensely difficult to rhyme well.

Caution

Poets have been rhyming in English for over six hundred years. New and refreshing rhymes are hard to come by. With some words the possibilities have worn extremely thin. One can rhyme *love* rather unoriginally with *dove, glove, above* or even *move*, but then one has just about had *enough*.

Also, full rhymes – like *love* and *glove*, *crank* and *spank* – tend to fall rather heavily in English. Because most of the obvious rhymes have been used a thousand times, and because of their tendency to thump, the effect of full rhymes can often be (unintentionally) comic. If the rhymes feel too familiar, you will almost inevitably sound as though you are imitating an older kind of poetry, and your poem will lose in authenticity.

Poems don't have to rhyme, and there are lots of other things we can do to give them shape and structure. Remember MILTON calling rhyme "the Invention of a barbarous Age, to set off wretched matter and lame Meeter". It is always better to rely on strong matter and confident, expressive metre, than on aching rhymes.

Rhyming Well

Having started on this cautionary note, the next thing to say is that good rhymes can be extremely effective. Everything depends on what the poem is trying to do. If it's trying to be funny, a thumping rhyme might work well. If it's trying to be clever, unusual rhymes could help.

The central question you have to ask is: do you want your rhymes to draw attention to themselves? – in which case thump them out loud. Or do you want them to add unobtrusively to the overall musical effect? – in which case find ways of softening them.

Softening Rhyme

Most of the time, you probably won't want your rhymes to claim the centre of attention in your poems. If you use them at all, you will want them to work for the poem, rather than against it. There are four good ways of softening the potentially thumping, attention-grabbing effect of rhymes in English.

Half-rhymes

One way is to make your rhymes suggestive rather than obvious. You can do this by using half-rhymes or near-rhymes. Instead of using the same vowel and consonant sounds, as in the full rhyme *walk* and *talk*, you can use the same vowels with different consonants, as in *flap* and *flag*, or *slow* and *control*. Alternatively, you can use the same consonant sounds with differing vowel sounds, as in *road* and *dead*, *milk* and *sulk*.

Word-length

Varying the length, in particular the number of syllables, between rhyming words can also soften the effect. *Slow* and *control* is already one example; others might be *scree* and *disconsolately*, *half* and *flagstaff*, *undress* and *emptiness*. Of course, you can also combine syllable variation with half-rhymes, as in *shapes* and *periscopes*, *engine* and *dizzying*.

Look at how L<small>ARKIN</small> makes use of rhymes based on syllable variation in the first stanza of "Home is so Sad" (1958), and half-rhymes in the second stanza:

Examples

Home is so sad. It stays as it was left,
Shaped to the comfort of the last to go
As if to win them back. Instead, bereft
Of anyone to please, it withers so,
Having no heart to put aside the theft

And turn again to what it started as,
A joyous shot at how things ought to be,
Long fallen wide. You can see how it was:
Look at the pictures and the cutlery.
The music in the piano stool. That vase.

L<small>ARKIN</small> is equally happy to make use of thumping full rhymes in a more (darkly) comic mood. Look at "This Be The Verse" from 1971:

They fuck you up, your mum and dad.
They may not mean to, but they do.
They fill you with the faults they had
And add some extra, just for you.

But they were fucked up in their turn
By fools in old-style hats and coats,
Who half the time were soppy-stern
And half at one another's throats.

Man hands on misery to man.
It deepens like a coastal shelf.
Get out as early as you can,
And don't have any kids yourself.

A third good way of softening rhymes is by making the sense of one line run on to the next. This is called *enjambment* or "running on". The opposite of a run-on line is an "end-stopped" one, in which the sense of a phrase is completed at the end of the line. The opening line of W<small>ALLACE</small> S<small>TEVENS</small>'<small>S</small> "Man Carrying Thing" cited in the previous chapter is a run-on line: "The poem must resist the intelligence / Almost successfully ...", whereas all the lines in L<small>AR-</small>KIN'<small>S</small> "This Be The Verse" are end-stopped, with the possible exception of line 5. Which lines run on in "Home is so Sad", and which are end-stopped? The way to tell is to see if you can make a slight pause in the voice at the end of the line. If you really can't, it's a run-on line. For me, the only line ending in the poem that won't tolerate any pause at all is line 3. The word "bereft" belongs to the phrase "of anyone to please", and "bereft of anyone to please" has to be spoken as a single, uninterrupted unit. This is precisely what takes the thump out of the rhyme *bereft* and *theft*.

Run-on Lines

Another Example	Read the following poem, "Sonnet", by EDWIN BROCK aloud.

It was a quiet night you will remember:
warm with a little mist between the trees:
we had left two children sleeping, the ease
of ten years loving was between. You were

in a broken mood, remember? I talked
as though I understood the world; the mist
between the trees, concealing lovers, kissed
our mood and pulled your hair uncurled. We walked

where we had been before we married; quiet
it was with my voice droning on; ten years
I talked away before I carried your mood
and you to where the grass was long, and tight
your love became to loose your worries,
as sweet your song becomes when I intrude.

Comment	This is a quiet and tender poem, although the last line reveals a disturbing dissonance beneath the tenderness. The metre is a loosely flowing iambic pentameter with plenty of variation to suggest the natural rhythms of ordinary speech. The rhymes are a mixture of soft half-rhymes (*remember* and *you were*; *quiet* and *tight*; *ten years* and *worries*), and very strong full ones (*trees* and *ease*; *mist* and *kissed*; *talked* and *walked*). There is also one syllable-variation rhyme (*mood* and *intrude*). The interesting thing about the full rhymes in this poem is that they all fall on run-on lines. As a result of this, we hardly hear them at all – even though they are veritable thumpers in themselves. This, of course, supports the gentle tone of the poem as a whole. The entire poem makes highly skilful and crafted use of rhyme.

Internal Rhyme	A fourth way of softening rhymes in poetry is to put the rhymes not at the ends of the lines, but somewhere in the middle. This is also a strategy used by EDWIN BROCK in "Sonnet". When we read the poem aloud, it is less the end-rhymes that we hear than the rhymes tucked away in the middle of other lines. Listen to the line-internal rhyme of *world* and *curled* in lines 6 and 8, and of *married* and *carried* in lines 9 and 11. The word *talked* at the beginning of line 11 is also a line-internal echo of the end-rhyme *walked* in line 8. And there is a subtle half-rhyme between *droning on* in line 10 and *long* in line 12, which itself rhymes fully with *song* in the middle of the last line.

Conclusion	Rhyme is great if you know how to use it. Used with the all the expertise displayed in "Sonnet", it can do wonders for a poem. Such expertise is the product of years of practice and hard work. It derives from a highly sophisticated ear, trained in close reading

and tireless experimentation. Always be on the look out for what other poets – of all ages – have achieved with rhyme, and never tire of trying out different things yourself.

An Exercise

Take fourteen rhyming words that follow the same rhyme scheme as EDWIN BROCK'S "Sonnet" (ABBA, CDDC, EFGEFG). Try to mix nouns and verbs, full rhymes and half-rhymes. You might take, for example, "good", "went", "spent", "food"; "despise", "tepid", "intrepid", "wise"; "loan", "make", "maroon"; "gown", "take", "soon". Put these rhyme words at the end of every line and build a poem around them. Try to make at least ten of the fourteen lines run-on lines.

4 The Rustle of Language

Music

De la musique avant tout chose, ("Be musical above all things") wrote VERLAINE in his "Art Poetique" at the end of the nineteenth century. The idea that music was the highest of the arts, and that poetry should aspire to emulate it, was a commonplace among the symbolists. But music has one freedom that language simply doesn't enjoy: its notes and pitches, harmonies and dissonances, keys and intervals, do not refer directly to things in the real world. Words do.

When we speak of the music of language – just as when we speak of the language of music – we are using a metaphor. This is not to say that the metaphor is bad – only that we should not forget that it is only a metaphor.

Pleasure

In EDWIN BROCK'S "Sonnet", several word-sounds are repeated, without necessarily rhyming. Just take the first stanza:

It was a quiet night you will remember:
warm with a little mist between the trees;
we had left two children sleeping, the ease
of ten years loving was between. You were ...

The words "quiet" and "night", in the first line, sound similar. The word "will" has the same vowel sound as "with", "little" and "mist" in line 2. There is the same "ee" sound in "between" and "trees" in line 2, and "sleeping" and "ease" in line 3; "between" is repeated in line 4, coming after "years" which also has a similar vowel sound. There are several soft "l" sounds and whispering "s" sounds in these first four lines.

These effects are pleasing in themselves. We do seem to take pleasure in the repetition and variation of formal elements in poetry, just as we do in music. The "sonic" repetitions and variations in BROCK'S "Sonnet" undoubtedly add to the mood conveyed by the meaning of the words themselves. This does not mean, however, that "ee"s and "l"s and "s"s necessarily convey a sense of softness or tenderness. "*She squealed like a bleating sheep as he slit her larynx with a rusty scalpel*". Doors can creak and seagulls can shriek without any suggestion of softness. And if we were simply to reproduce the sounds of Brock's poem, without the same meaning, (Shit caused a fly at night to kill a member") no one would say we had written anything terribly beautiful. Sound can support sense, but the sense always comes first.

Devices

Once we have recognised these two important principles – that sound patterns can be pleasing in themselves, but they are most pleasing when they are informed by meaning – we can start looking at various devices that can be used effectively to yoke sound to sense. In addition to metre and rhyme, the three best known are *alliteration*, *assonance*, and *onomatopoeia*. Examples of all four can be found in the excerpt from Pope's *An Essay on Criticism* cited at the beginning of this chapter.

Alliteration

Alliteration is the repetition of consonant sounds at the beginning of a series of neighbouring words, as in tongue-twisters like "Peter Piper picked a peck of pickled pepper" or "she sells sea shells by the sea shore". When consonant sounds are repeated after different vowels (as in sip and sup, clip and clop, creak and croak) we speak of *consonance*. Pope makes use of alliteration in the line "The sound must seem an echo to the sense", and both alliteration and consonance in describing winds and rivers: "Soft is the strain when Zephyr gently blows, / And the smooth stream in smoother numbers flows".

Assonance

Assonance is the repetition of vowel sounds like the "ee"s in the first four lines of Brock's "Sonnet". In a highly recommendable book on *Writing Poems*, Peter Sansom shows how Ted Hughes puts both alliteration and assonance to good use in his poem "Wind". The poem is a rush of motion, but there is an impressive moment when a gull is described trying to hold his ground:

The wind flung a magpie away and a black-
Back gull bent like an iron bar slowly...

Commenting on the repetition of consonants "b" and "l", and the vowels "a" and "i", Sansom writes: "You have no option, reading that aloud, but to have the words put their back into it." He adds: "There is a modulation too in 'slowly' which has a longer, slower vowel sound. These [devices] do make a difference of course to the way we read – and scan – and indeed *understand* the line." (Sansom 1994: 82)

Onomatopoeia is the use of words to imitate sounds. Thus, in "God's Grandeur", GERARD MANLEY HOPKINS speaks of the "ooze of oil" and of generations of heavy feet that "have trod, have trod, have trod", and TENNYSON, in "The Princess", describes the "murmuring of innumerable bees". POPE, in our excerpt, uses a combination of "s" "sh" and "r" sounds very effectively to evoke the breaking of waves: "But when loud *surges* la*sh* the *s*ounding *sh*ore, / The hoar*s*e *r*ough *ve*r*se *sh*ould like the torrent *r*oar*".

Once again, we need to remember that sound follows sense. There is no simple one-to-one correlation between the words we use to imitate sounds and the actual sounds themselves. Just think of how different languages imitate the same animal noises. English ducks "quack", Danish ducks "rap" and Japanese ducks simply go "gaga".

Onomato-poeia

In Chapter 5, I suggested that you listen to sounds in the world around you and try finding real or nonsense words with which to imitate them. If you've already jotted some sounds down in your notebook, go back to them now. If not, go out and listen for an afternoon to the street, the park, the station, the bus, the café – writing down a list of words that you feel effectively imitate the sounds you hear.

Try, additionally, to write a list of onomatopoetic words to evoke the sound of the following:

Exercise

- running water,
- a coffee-grinder
- someone typing on a keyboard
- a car driven with a flat tyre
- the air brakes of a bus or lorry
- the echoes in a swimming baths.

Think up further lists of your own.

Now write a poem of four lines in which you use some of your onomatopoeic words to suggest to the reader the sounds you are seeking to imitate. When you are happy that the poem works, try something different. In another four-line poem, use the same words to suggest very different sounds. That is to say, if in the first poem you used your onomatopoeic words to evoke the sound of a lawn mower, try in the second poem to get the same sounds to suggest birdsong or laughter.

CHAPTER Writing Poems: Form and Finish

Focus

So far we have been thinking in terms of feet and rhymes and sounds and lines. Now we are going to start working with whole poems. We'll begin with a very simple form then go on to more complex ones. After looking at form, we'll turn to questions of finishing: stepping back, revising, and improving.

❶ Working with Form

Form

Form is a friend. Used well, with imagination and craft, it is an enabler and not a constraint. It helps to give shape to our ideas, rather than squeezing them into a straitjacket. It takes time and a good deal of hard work to make form work for you and not against you. Poetry is a craft, and you have to learn to use the tools of the trade. Sure, we write poems to express (and explore) our thoughts and feeling and ideas. But these thoughts and feelings and ideas are rather wobbly puddings without form. They are not very appetizing or satisfying to others. Form can give the products of our imagination a life of their own, help them stand on their own two feet. It can also help us to say things that, without it, we might never have known we knew.

Haiku

Economy

A haiku is a very short poem and a good form to start practising in. It is three lines long and consists of a total of seventeen syllables. There are five syllables in the first line, seven in the second, and five in the third. Because the haiku is so short, words have to be used with great economy. You only have seventeen syllables, so not one can be wasted. The cultivation of this kind of discipline will benefit all your poetry.

History

The haiku is a Japanese lyric form that emerged in the sixteenth century and became highly popular in the centuries that followed. One of its most famous practitioners was MATSUO BASHO (1644–94), whose haiku are predominately intensely atmospheric, miniature snapshots of the natural world. In Western poetry, the haiku became particularly influential at the beginning of the twentieth century, largely through the work of the American and British "Imagists", such as EZRA POUND, H.D., and AMY LOWELL. Haiku tend to be concrete and imagistic. Often, two discrete images are yoked together to evoke a particular, unexpected mood. EZRA POUND called haiku "a form of super-position ... one idea set on top of another." Some poets have also written purely "ideational" haiku: using the form to express paradoxes, conundrums and conceits, rather than images and atmospheres.

Here are translations of two traditional Japanese haiku, the first by BASHO, the second by MORITAKE:

Examples

In the autumn wind
lies, sorrowfully broken,
a mulberry stick.

The falling flower
I saw drift back to the branch
was a butterfly.

The Imagists tended to be pretty free with the number of syllables they used in their haiku. Here are two haiku-type poems by EZRA POUND:

O fan of white silk,
clear as frost on the grass-blade,
You are also laid aside.

> *In a Station of the Metro*

The apparition of these faces in the crowd;
Petals on a wet, black bough.

And here are two idea-based haiku by PETER PORTER:

Told today's music
is HMV Positive,
they practice safe sound.

Yes, yes, yes, yes, yes.
The correct translation reads
no, no, no, no, no.

Before you start writing haiku, try to feel the pulse of the syllabic lines: ta-ta-ta-ta-ta / ta-ti-ta-ti-ta-ti-ta / ta-ta-ta-ta-ta. Drum the syllable pattern out with your fingers, starting at the thumb. Once you have the pattern in your head, you hardly have to count syllables at all when you come to write.

Pulse

Start off with very imagistic haiku. Keep the language as concrete as possible. No abstract words, and no stated feelings. Let the detail of the images carry the weight of any emotion you want to express.

Images

When you feel you have got the hang of writing single haiku, have a go at writing a cycle of seven. Take as your theme: "Stone".

Cycles

The most important lesson to be learnt from writing haiku is economy and concreteness of expression. These lessons will serve you well in other forms, too.

The following exercise explores a way of extending a haiku-like stanza into a longer poem. It can be done alone, but it is best done in pairs.

Exercise

Take as your theme: a wall. Write a haiku-type poem, but this time, instead of writing only three lines, write four. The first line should be five syllables, the second and third lines seven syllables, and the fourth line five syllables (5, 7, 7, 5). Remember to keep the images concrete and to avoid abstractions and the explicit statement of feelings.

If you are working in pairs, now exchange poems. If you are working alone just carry on with your own four-liner.

Add another four lines of 5, 7, 7, 5 syllables to the ones you have been given. The new four lines should add to or expand upon the first four. Remember to stay in haiku style the whole time, concrete and economical.

When you are ready, exchange poems again. Look carefully at the eight lines in front of you and try to see the direction the poem is taking. This time, don't simply continue the idea, but leave a single space on the page and add a twist, an unexpected turn of events or change of mood. Use only three lines, and use the traditional haiku syllable pattern: 5, 7, 5. You are not finishing the poem yet, so it is possible to leave things open.

Now swap poems for the last time. Add to the eleven lines already completed one final three-line haiku with 5, 7, 5, syllables. This haiku must remain, like all the others, tight and concrete, but it must at the same time clearly bring the poem to a close.

Comment

Stand back and look at what you have written. You should have fourteen lines with a turn in direction or mood in the ninth line. Yes, you guessed it – you are already on your way to writing a sonnet.

The Sonnet

The Form

The sonnet (from *sonetto*, "little song") is a poem of fourteen lines. In English poetry it has traditionally – but far from exclusively – been written in iambic pentameter, or at least with lines of between 10 and 12 syllables. The form originated in Sicily in the thirteenth century, and was made popular throughout Europe by PETRARCH (FRANCESCO PETRARCA, 1304–74) in the fourteenth. There are two main varieties of the sonnet in English poetry: the *Italian* (or *Petrarchan*) sonnet and the *English* (or *Shakespearean*) sonnet.

The Italian sonnet consists of two major parts: an *octave* (the first eight lines), and a *sestet* (the last six lines). Between the two, there is generally a "turn" in direction, meaning or mood, as there was in our haiku-sonnet. The octave can further be broken down into two quatrains, and the sestet into two tercets. This structure is reflected in the rhyme scheme of the Italian sonnet: ABBA; ABBA; CDE; CDE.

This form was introduced into English poetry in the sixteenth century by SIR THOMAS WYATT, who both translated and imitated the sonnets of PETRARCH.

Italian

The English sonnet consists of three quatrains and a final couplet. It rhymes: ABAB; CDCD; EFEF; GG. This structure tends to encourage a "turn" after the first twelve lines (or *douzain*). Many English sonnets, however – including many of SHAKESPEARE'S – also turn after line eight (see, for example, SHAKESPEARE'S Sonnet 18).

The form was introduced into English poetry by HENRY HOWARD, the EARL OF SURREY, who also translated PETRARCH, but changed the structure of the sonnet in doing so. Have a look at WYATT'S "The longe love that in my thought doeth harbar" and SURREY'S "Love that doth raine and live within my thought", two very different translations of the same PETRARCH poem.

SHAKESPEARE used SURREY'S "English" form for his great cycle of sonnets written at the turn of the sixteenth and seventeenth centuries. It is SHAKESPEARE'S magnificent cycle of sonnets that gives the English form its other widely used name.

English

This basic description of sonnet forms is all very well as far as it goes; but it doesn't go very far. The sonnet-ness of the sonnet doesn't reside merely in its fourteen lines, its octaves and sestets or douzains and couplets, and its English or Italian rhymes. The sonnet is the sum of what can be done with these formal elements; it is a living, breathing thing, a thought that grows and develops, a journey that takes you somewhere new. The structures of the sonnet are the means that give it life; they are not the life itself.

All the same, one of the great pleasures of working with sonnets is that they have a way of shaping ideas and making them happen. What at first sight appear to be severe technical restrictions turn out to be powerful stimulants to the imagination. WORDSWORTH actually wrote a sonnet about just that ("Nuns Fret Not").

The Point of Form

I find the form of the Italian sonnet particularly suggestive. Just take that central ratio of octave to sestet, eight to six. This is very close to the mathematical ratio known as the Golden Section, which plays an important role in several of the arts – in landscape painting, for example, (the ratio of land to sky), in architecture and in music. And try this little piece of mathematics: halve the sonnet; divide eight and six by two and you have four and three.

Numbers

Then multiply them by ten and you have forty and thirty. Add these two numbers together and you have seventy, three score and ten, the biblical lifespan of a human being.

Whatever else an Italian sonnet is about, it's also partly about the experience of turning forty. In the octave of your life you still have all the time in the world. You can try out this idea or image and then that simile or metaphor. Suddenly you get to the turn, and there are only six lines – thirty years – left. The time remaining is less than the time you have already spent; you have already used up more than half your resources. The sestet has to be more intense, more economical. You still have everything to say, but only six more lines to say it in.

Reading

While you work through this section on sonnets, read as many published sonnets as you can. The Elizabethan Age was particularly rich in sonnet writing; in addition to those of SHAKESPEARE, WYATT and SURREY, you should at least look at some by SIR PHILIP SIDNEY and EDMUND SPENSER. SPENSER added a modification to the form, by rhyming his sonnets ABAB; BCBC: CDCD; EE. MILTON wrote powerful sonnets, as did many of the Romantics, especially SHELLEY, KEATS and WORDSWORTH (who wrote over 500). The sonnets of the Victorian poet GERARD MANLEY HOPKINS are extraordinary explorations of effusive sound and complex sense (try "The Windhover"). Nearly all the best poets of the twentieth century tried their hands at sonnets, and the form is very much alive today. There are several good anthologies of sonnets you can turn to. Both Oxford and Penguin, for example, have brought out major collections in the last few years.

Exercises

In the following exercises, we'll take a pretty broad view of the sonnet and do some experimentation with the form. Sonnets don't have to rhyme (WALLACE STEVENS and ROBERT LOWELL have written some magnificent unrhymed sonnets); they don't even have to have fourteen lines (GEORGE MEREDITH'S *Modern Love*, 1862, is a cycle of sixteen-line sonnets, a form revived more recently by the poet TONY HARRISON). In order still to be sonnets, however, these variations have to bear some relation to the basic form. In those exercises below which involve diverging from the traditional sonnet form, the poems should still retain a "sonnety" feel.

Rhymes
First 1.

We have already done a version of this exercise earlier in Chapter 6. We took fourteen rhyming words to the rhyme-scheme of EDWIN BROCK'S "Sonnet". Now try doing the same with an English sonnet. Think of fourteen rhyming words to the pattern ABAB, CDCD; EFEF; GG: for example: strange, garden, rearrange, pardon; so, uncle, go, carbuncle; mission, suitcase, vision, fruitcake; not, rot. Put these rhymes at the end of each line and write an English sonnet around them. Write, if possible, in iambic pentameter, or at least try to stick to a five-pulse line. Think carefully about where you want end-stopped lines and where you want to run on. Remember, run-on lines will make the rhymes less obvious. Also, think very carefully about your last rhyme (G, G), the final couplet. What do you want your couplet to do? Does it sum up or comment on what has already been said, or does it offer a new twist?

Try the same exercise with either an Italian or another English sonnet, but this time vary the length of each line. At least one line should only be one word long, i. e., should contain only the rhyme word. CHRISTOPHER REID does something along these lines in his sonnet "Fly". The poem is a mixture of English and Italian patterns (and the shortest lines are three words long, whereas your shortest line should be just one word):

Rhymes First 2.

A fat fly fuddles for an exit
at the window pane.
Bluntly, stubbornly, inspects it,
like a brain
nonplussed by a seemingly simple sentence
in a book,
which the glaze of unduly protracted acquaintance
has turned to gobbledygook.

A few inches above where the fly fizzes
a gap of air
waits, but this has
not yet been vouchsafed to the fly.
Only retreat and a loop or swoop of despair
will give it the sky.

Have a look at some Elizabethan sonnets. Find one that really interests you and try to re-set it in a modern context and rewrite it for a modern readership. It's entirely up to you if you want to use regular rhyme and metre. But do try to make the poem sound and feel like "now" and not like the product of an earlier century. Have a look WENDY COPE's cycle called *Strugnell's Sonnets*. Look also at MICHAEL HULSE's "The Critics are too much with us", a reworking of WORDSWORTH's sonnet, "The World is too much with us".

Resetting

So far we've only considered two basic ways of mapping out the movement of sonnets on the page. There's the Italian pattern of eight lines and six lines (or two sets of four lines and two sets of three) and the English douzain and couplet (or three groups of four lines and one group of two). There are, of course, endless ways of varying these patterns. One might begin with a couplet, or a sestet, or a tercet. One might write a whole sonnet in couplets (rhyming or unrhyming). You might try four stanzas of three lines

Units of Thought

each and a couplet to end. Or one line in the first stanza, two in the second, three in the fourth, and four in the fifth and sixth. Experiment with as many variations as possible. Always ask yourself: what kind of thought do the units support? What ideas work well in couplets, and how does the breathing of the poem change when written in units of three lines? Use these experiments to find the right patterns for the right ideas.

Nets

Have a go at writing half-sonnets, "sons" or "nets". Try seven lines with a turn after line four. Make the lines about half as long as a full iambic pentameter line. Try, for example, a pattern like this:

```
v / v / v /
v / v /
v / v /
v / v / v /

v / v /
v / v / v /
v / v /
```

The Sestina

Form

The sestina, an invention of the troubadour poets, is a complex form made up of six stanzas of six lines each, and a three-line *envoi* ("send-off") at the end. The words which end the six lines of the first stanza are also used in all five subsequent stanzas, only in a different order. This sets considerable constraints upon the poem, but also opens up all sorts of possibilities of invention. The pattern often forces you to say things you hadn't anticipated saying. The best way to understand how a sestina works is to look at an example. Here is a famous one by ELIZABETH BISHOP. It is from 1965 and is simply called "Sestina":

September rain falls on the house.
In the failing light, the old grandmother
sits in the kitchen with the child
beside the Little Marvel Stove,
reading the jokes from the almanac,
laughing and talking to hide her tears.

She thinks that her equinoctial tears
and the rain that beats on the roof of the house
were both foretold by the almanac,
but only known to a grandmother.
The iron kettle sings on the stove.
She cuts some bread and says to the child,

It's time for tea now; but the child
is watching the teakettle's small hard tears
dance like mad on the hot black stove,
the way the rain must dance on the house.
Tidying up, the old grandmother
hangs up the clever almanac

on its string. Birdlike, the almanac
hovers half open above the child,
hovers above the old grandmother
and her teacup full of dark brown tears.
She shivers and says she thinks the house
feels chilly, and puts more wood in the stove.

It was to be, says the Marvel Stove.
I know what I know, says the almanac.
With crayons the child draws a rigid house
and a winding pathway. Then the child
puts in a man with buttons like tears
and shows it proudly to the grandmother.

But secretly, while the grandmother
busies herself about the stove,
the little moons fall down like tears
from between the pages of the almanac
into the flower bed the child
has carefully placed in the front of the house.

Time to plant tears, says the almanac.
The grandmother sings to the marvelous stove
and the child draws another inscrutable house.

Can you see the pattern the repetition of the end-words makes in this poem? Number the end-words on the basis of the first stanza and you get: 1 house, 2 grandmother, 3 child, 4 stove, 5 almanac, and 6 tears. If the order of the first stanza, then, is 123456, the second stanza is 615243, the third 364152, the fourth 532614, the fifth 451362, and the sixth 246531. The logic is this: each stanza takes the last end-word of the previous stanza as its first end-word, the first end-word of the previous stanza as its second end-word, the fifth as its third, the second as its fourth, the fourth as its fifth and the third as its sixth.

Pattern

Each line of the *envoi* repeats two of the end-words – one in the middle of the line and one at the end. In Bishop's "Sestina", the end-words used in the first line of the envoi are 6 and 5, in the second 2 and 4, and in the third 3 and 1.

Hearing all this, you probably feel like saying what Byron said about Robert Southey at the beginning of *Don Juan*: "I wish he would explain his explanations". Actually it's almost easier to write a (bad) sestina than to explain how one works.

Advantages

Even if the sestina is not as complicated as it sounds, you might still wonder why anyone should want to write one. Why take so much rope with so many knots in it just to go and hang yourself?

Three answers come immediately to mind. First, the seemingly rigid structure of the sestina is not so much an obstacle as an aid to composition. Once the end-word structure is in place, you'll find that much of the poem wants to write itself around it. Secondly, the repeated end-words are an excellent substitute for rhyme. With judicious use of run-on lines, you certainly don't notice them as thumping repetitions. They work more like echoes and memories. Thirdly, they give you an opportunity to open up the meanings of words. Try to choose end-words that have more than one meaning so that you can explore different senses nearly every time they appear in new contexts.

Exercise

Have a go at writing a sestina. Don't worry about keeping a regular metre unless you particularly want one (traditionally, sestinas tend to be in iambic tetrameter or pentameter). First time round, don't think about your end-words, just write six lines and use the end-words that come for the rest of the poem. Save a careful choice of end-words for your second sestina. Use your first sestina as a way of generating ideas, not as a way of whipping them into shape.

Try to make every line as natural as possible. Avoid inversions and unidiomatic syntax. Make new senses of the end-words by running them on in different ways and contexts. The more natural your phrasing is, the less obvious it should be to the reader that s/he is reading a sestina at all.

Reading

The sestina seems to be back in fashion. Have a look at BISHOP'S "Sestina", ANTHONY HECHT'S "The Book of Yolek", JOHN ASHBERRY'S "The Painter" and "Farm Implements and Rutabagas in a Landscape", and PATIENCE AGBABI'S "Seven Sisters" a series of seven sestinas – all using the same end-words! – in her collection *Transformatrix* (2000).

Free Verse

Costly Liberties

There's nothing much to say about "free verse" except to echo T. S. ELIOT'S dictum that good verse is never free. Free verse is simply poetry without the constraints of rhyme and regular metre. But it still makes use of other devices in order to be verse at all. Line breaks, for example, are never "free"; they are, for a poem, a matter of life and death. Anyone who sees "free verse" as an easy option is suffering under an illusion. As PETER SANSOM puts it in *Writing Poems*: "Writing free verse is 'easier' than using a fixed form, in that it takes less effort to write bad free verse than a bad villanelle."

② Finishing

When is a poem finished? Presumably, when every word sits, when not a single sound, image, idea or sentiment can possibly be added or taken away. How are we to know when this is the case? In some instances it's obvious; the poem just shouts up at you from the page: there, that's it! Mostly, however, finishing is a fiddly business. Something that seemed just perfect at two o'clock in the morning, may seem a long way from perfect after breakfast the following day. You need to be able to step back, give yourself time, and revise with absolute rigour.

Focus

It is easy to fall in love with our creations while they are still hot from the pen or buzzing from the furious tapping of computer keys. It is easy to confuse the pleasure of simply having got something done with the pleasure afforded by a thing done well. But at some point, we have to look again at our work from a more critical distance. And the first ingredient of this distance is time. When you think you've finished a poem, put it away for a couple of weeks and come back to it with fresh eyes. WORDSWORTH is famous for having called poetry "the overflow of spontaneous emotions"; but he added the proviso: "recollected in tranquility". Give yourself time to develop the tranquility to review your spontaneity with a critical eye and ear.

Time

Speaking of ears, always read your poetry aloud – at every stage of composition. Your ears may be able to spot things missed by your eyes. If even you stumble over a line, there is almost certainly something wrong with it.

Reading Aloud

Try to read what you have written as if you were a complete stranger. You have no idea about the background to the poem and all the work that went into it. You have no particular emotional stake in what happens to the dead cat, or the lonely aunt, or the windswept post-season seaside resort in question. It's not your cat or aunt, and you don't even know where Billingsbogbow-on-Sea is. Would you really bother to read the poem at all? Try to think of three good reasons why someone who isn't you should read your poem. If you can't think of one, either the poem isn't yet finished, or it's just for you alone.

Reading as Another

A second Opinion

Only show your poem to someone else when you have already tried to read it *as* someone else. Showing poems too early can be counterproductive. The same is often true of talking to others about poems before they are well on the way to being finished. Writing a poem is always an exploratory process, and it is very easy to lose the tension of discovery by prematurely letting the cat out of the bag.

Once you've got the cat out on your own, however, and you know what colour it is, and what kind of tail it has, it is, of course, crucial to have it looked at by another felaphile. Be aware of whom you are showing your work to. Some friends tend to like the things we write because they like us. Try to show your work to people who read contemporary poetry, avidly and critically. Listen carefully to what they say. If they stumble over details you yourself were unsure of, this is a good sign that something has to be changed. If they loathe the very bits of the poem that you like best, there's very little you can do. At the end of the day, it's your poem.

Revising

Nearly all good work is the product of careful rewriting. A poem that is going to stand up to the scrutiny of others and give them pleasure rarely comes out reader-ready first time. Revising often means learning to let go of details that are dear to you. BOSWELL quotes SAMUEL JOHNSON quoting the advice of a college tutor: "Read over your compositions and where ever you meet a passage which you think is particularly fine, strike it out." Sometimes a phrase or image may be superb, but not quite right for the poem you've put it in.

Pruning

Most writers, new and experienced, tend to try to do too much in a first draft and end up cutting. Less can often be more, as PETER SANSOM points out in the following example:

At the end of a poem called "The Vase", for instance, we might get: "It slipped from my hands". An indifferent poet would add "and smashed to pieces", and a bad one would add to that, "It could never be mended". But it would take a terrible poet to go on with: "That vase was my life [/our relationship/a symbol of the delicate ecological balance] and now it is shards." (SANSOM 1994: 41)

Never worry about cutting. We prune trees to make them grow better. Trust your own imagination. Whatever you get rid of, there's always plenty more where that came from, and even when you have to start again from scratch, nothing ever goes entirely wasted. I remember attending one workshop in which, after everyone had spent about forty minutes on an exercise, someone came round with a rubbish bin and collected our work. We all wondered what would happen next, but that was the end of the exercise. Our texts were thrown away and we never saw them again. The point was to get us used to parting with cherished ideas and to starting all over again.

❸ Extending

If you've just finished revising a poem and found yourself pruning a lot of details that you are reluctant to jettison, it may just be that you have material for more than one poem. It may be that you have the makings of a whole cycle of poems.

Cuttings

Thinking in cycles can take a great deal of weight off the shoulders of a single poem. You don't have to pack all your ideas in at once. This will help you to let your poems breathe. Often enough, the constellation of concerns that triggers our writing is not exhausted by a single poem.

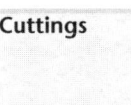
Cycles

Some ideas can themselves suggest cycles of poems. I remember standing on the Rialto Bridge in Venice on an overcast morning in spring. Suddenly I noticed that lights were flashing endlessly from both banks of the Grand Canal. I was having my photograph taken by hundreds of tourists. I stood there for about five minutes wondering how many people in how many different parts of the world would have a photograph of the Rialto Bridge on their mantelpieces, with me standing right in the middle. How many completely different and separate lives, all linked by a single, trivial, common detail: they all have a photograph of me in their living rooms.

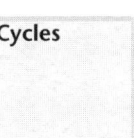
Cyclic Ideas

Try writing a series of poems about very different people who all share something small and utterly arbitrary in common. You might observe a particular table at a café during the course of an afternoon and catch snippets of conversation from all the different people who sit there. Try basing six poems on six separate snippets from the conversations of six separate couples.

Exercises

Or stand at the bottom of a stairway – in a station, outside a public building, in a multi-storey car park. Watch people coming down. Ask yourself where they have been and where they are going. What is on their minds? Choose five cases that interest you and write five poems.

As you write, allow new connections to emerge. Perhaps there is more that links these various lives than you had initially imagined.

Whether or not you intend to write cycles, it is always interesting to try to group your poems. Some poems read very differently when set beside others. Look at the way poets group their poems

Grouping

in individual volumes of their poetry. How do these groupings affect the way we read? Whether or not you wish to produce a volume of your own poetry, grouping poems will tell you a lot about your own interests and concerns. Do you always write about the same things? Wouldn't it be good to try something different? It is surprising just how liberating it can be to write against the grain. Sometimes, the best pieces come from trying something entirely new.

Explore

Finally, never stop experimenting. We are confronted all the time with the reality of what the poet LOUIS MACNIECE called "the drunkenness of things being various". Like the world around us, we are changing all the time. Our poems will want to change, too. Different types of experience will require different forms of response. Poetry is not so much an account of the world as an exploration of our ever-changing experience of it. Keep going. Keep trying out new tools and ideas. Try rhyming if you don't usually rhyme. Try a long poem if you usually write short ones. And keep reading poetry. Get yourself a good anthology like *The Norton Anthology of Poetry* or the excellent *New Penguin Book of English Verse*. Above all, read as much contemporary poetry as you can lay your hands on.

Creative Writing and the University

CHAPTER

This chapter differs from all the other chapters of this book. It offers reflections on Creative Writing as a university subject, as opposed to providing practical exercises in Creative Writing. Nevertheless, some of the basic ideas which inform the practical approach to writing taken throughout this book are spelt out in this chapter and I hope it will be of interest to all practitioners of Creative Writing, including students and teachers.

The chapter makes a case for the value of Creative Writing in the broader context of the university study of English. It focuses first and foremost on the potential of Creative Writing as a part of university English studies in an environment in which English is not the native language.

Focus

1 What is Creative Writing?

Creative Writing is an odd term, and many of the best teachers of, and campaigners for, the subject have long been unhappy with some of the implications the term seems to suggest. Surely any good writing is creative – from catchy advertising copy to a lively and entertaining letter or a well-formulated student essay. The problem with the term "creative" is that it suggests, in many people's minds at least, an opposition with "critical". This is an opposition that any self-respecting book or course on Creative Writing will want to challenge. Good critical thinking and writing are inevitably creative, just as any good creative writing is inevitably critical. To produce a good sonnet (or sestina, or short story) you have to be a highly critical – and above all self-critical – user of language. A decent sonnet is never merely the product of momentary inspiration. It requires a sophisticated critical understanding of the form and a keen awareness of the way it has developed in literary history. Good creative writers are by definition demanding critical readers and, often enough, highly discerning literary critics. This was as true of SIR PHILIP SIDNEY in the sixteenth century as of JOHN DRYDEN, ALEXANDER POPE, SAMUEL JOHNSON, SAMUEL TAYLOR COLERIDGE, PERCY BYSSHE SHELLEY, HENRY JAMES, VIRGINIA WOOLF, EZRA POUND, T.S. ELIOT, WALLACE STEVENS, and PAUL MULDOON – just to cite a handful of obvious examples – in the centuries that followed. Creative Writing is a serious cerebral business.

The Term

History

Creative Writing, as a critical, intellectual activity, has been taught at university level for over a hundred years. Ultimately, it derives from the composition courses offered at Harvard University in the United States in the 1880s. A decisive moment in its institutional history came in 1928, when the University of Iowa agreed to accept Creative Writing work as part of the submissions for advanced degrees. Out of this decision grew the "Iowa Writers' Workshop" and the beginnings of postgraduate Creative Writing teaching in US universities.

In Great Britain, it is only in the last thirty odd years that Creative Writing has really taken off as a university discipline. A pioneering role in this development has been played by the Creative Writing M.A. programme of the University of East Anglia in Norwich, still probably the most prestigious Creative Writing course in the UK. The programme was initiated by two major British writers, MALCOLM BRADBURY and ANGUS WILSON, in 1970. When the course was first offered in 1970, there was only one student, who met his two tutors in pubs and teashops in Norwich. That student was IAN MCEWAN, who went on to become one of the most important British novelists of his generation. Later students of the course have also become highly successful writers, with KAZUO ISHIGURO, CLIVE SINCLAIR and ROSE TREMAIN among the best known.

Today, most university English departments in the UK offer courses in Creative Writing in one form or another at undergraduate and postgraduate level. Some, including the University of East Anglia, even offer a PhD in Creative Writing.

Beyond the Anglophone Environment

Outside the UK and the USA, however, Creative Writing continues to meet with considerable suspicion, if not scorn, in the academy. Creative Writing courses are often perceived to be subjective, unscholarly, and academically irrelevant – a bit like community evening classes in knitting, pottery or underwater-archery. It's all very well for cranks, old ladies and lovesick teenagers, but …. This chapter will challenge these preconceptions by making a case for the intellectual rigour and academic value of Creative Writing as a serious university discipline.

Creative Writing in a Second Language

Another problem with the term Creative Writing is that it tends to mean different things in different national and institutional contexts. Many British and North American Creative Writing postgraduate courses see their primary aim as the training of professional writers. This cannot be the central aim when teaching Creative Writing in a non-native speaker context. Writers like NABOKOV and BECKETT, who wrote equally memorably in a first and second language, belong to a pretty rare species. Plenty of other great writers have not come close to matching their achievement: T.S. ELIOT and RAINER MARIA RILKE both wrote poetry in French, and

W.H. AUDEN tried his hand at sonnets in German, but, thankfully, these are not the works they are remembered for.

Teaching Creative Writing in English Studies in a non-Anglophone context necessarily has to be about something else. Above all it has to do with the practical appreciation of the language and literature being studied.

SAMUEL BECKETT started writing in French at least partly because he didn't like the noises that came out when he wrote in his native language. English came so easily that the words he wrote didn't sound as if they were his own. He looked for his own voice in the challenge of adopting a foreign tongue. Later, he returned to English, and the English he wrote was strange, distinctive, unique: that unmistakable BECKETT voice.

Home-comings

The experience of Creative Writing in a foreign tongue needs to be part a journey towards the rediscovery of the possibilities of one's own language. The most accomplished Creative Writing students I have had at the University of Cologne have almost all gone on to write their best work in German and some of that work has been published. All too often one hears students saying that it's easier to write in English than in German. Unfortunately this is generally because they don't hear all the overtones and resonances of their writing in a foreign language – things that will possibly strike a native ear as stilted or clichéd. It is precisely because one does hear these resonances in one's own language that writing in one's own language remains the more serious challenge. Students who are not interested in the potential of their native language will rarely write well in any other language either.

2 Creative Writing and the Study of Language and Literature

Writing fictional, poetic and dramatic texts and getting together with others to improve them is an eminently worthwhile activity in itself. It is also an activity that has a valuable contribution to make to other areas of literature and language study. In this section we shall briefly look at the value of Creative Writing in four key areas of English Studies: language learning; the development of rhetorical and communication skills; pedagogical development; and, perhaps most important of all, the appreciation and understanding of literature.

Focus

Language Learning

Registers
Student writing at university level tends to be somewhat limited when it comes to register. The type of language used in scholarly writing on literature and linguistics is fairly specialized and homogeneous. Creative Writing allows students to explore a far wider idiomatic range. Forms of language usage encountered passively in reading can be actively put to use in imaginative written work.

Language Areas
Creative Writing exercises can also be dovetailed to focus on particular areas of language learning. Short stories can be written around particular lexical fields, while story beginnings can provide a very useful way into questions of verbal *aspect*. Students might be asked, for example, to consider the difference between a story that begins "Someone was knocking at the door" and one that begins "Someone knocked at the door."

Process
Most writing at the university is end-product oriented. What counts is the final, submitted version of an essay, and not the process of thinking, writing, and rewriting that led up to it. In Creative Writing, this process aspect is of far greater importance. Rewriting is absolutely of the essence, and work can be repeatedly discussed at various stages.

Rhetorical and Communication Skills

Vocational Value
It is beginning to be more widely recognized that there is a potentially highly valuable vocational side to the study of Creative Writing. In what kind of job (outside of the academy) will graduates be called upon to produce a scholarly article with footnotes and a bibliography? The skills learnt in Creative Writing, on the other hand, are directly relevant to a wide range of professional activities from advertising to web writing.

Speed
In Creative Writing courses, students learn to think and formulate on the spot. Many writing exercises are performed against the clock. The idea is not to produce polished and publishable pieces of writing, but to get used to tapping imaginative resources quickly and effectively. The ability to come up with innovative ideas fast is an ability highly valued in the world of work.

Combination
Many classic Creative Writing exercises involve the convincing combination of apparently disconnected ideas. One simple beginner's exercise, for example, involves writing the name of an animal on one piece of paper and a domestic space on another. The animal is given to a neighbour on the left, the domestic space to

a neighbour on the right. Each participant then writes a three-line poem explaining what the animal they have been given is doing in the given domestic space. Of course, you are no more likely to be asked to write three-line animal poems in the world of work than you will be asked to write scholarly essays. However, the ability to combine discrete ideas and package them into a new convincing whole will be highly relevant to a range of professional challenges.

Creative Writing and the Teaching Situation

Creative Writing courses produce a different kind of group dynamic from other academic courses. The whole idea of a workshop is not only to improve one's own work, but to help others improve theirs. Much of one's time in a Creative Writing workshop is spent discussing texts by others, offering carefully considered, constructive advice.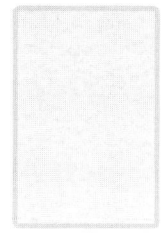

Workshops

Another great pedagogical value of Creative Writing workshops is that they teach students how to listen and respond to criticism. In few other courses will students find their work so regularly and so meticulously scrutinized. Much learning work also goes into the very tricky but important skill of giving constructive criticism. The ability to both offer and listen to constructive criticism is a skill that has enormous value beyond the workshop.

Criticism

Again, the process aspect of Creative Writing has considerable pedagogical value. In the evaluation of Creative Writing work, the final product need only be seen as the icing on the cake. Real achievement in writing has as much to do with becoming self-critical, recognizing weaknesses and working on them, as it has to do with producing a finished piece of work.

Achieve-ment

This process-oriented approach to achievement encourages many students to produce work of unexpectedly high quality. Students who have not necessarily been doing well in their academic writing may suddenly find that they are able to improve their writing skills in a Creative Writing workshop and that their new-found confidence works its way back into other areas of their academic work.

The workshop situation also presents a valuable pedagogical challenge to the teacher. The teacher does not preside over the group as a fount of specialized knowledge, but actively participates as a facilitator of constructive critical discussion. The altered relation between teacher and student fostered by the workshop experience can have a very positive effect on student-teacher interaction in other courses.

Teaching

Creative Writing as a Mode of Literary Understanding

Learning by Doing

In addition to being a fully justifiable intellectual activity in itself, for students of literature the practice of Creative Writing clearly has a very important role to play in the appreciation of literary forms, strategies and styles. One of the best ways of understanding how a thing works is to try making one oneself. This is as true for sonnets and short stories as it is for electronic circuits and chemical reactions.

EZRA POUND once wrote: "If you wanted to know something about an automobile, would you go to a man who had made one and driven it, or to a man who had merely heard about it?" Or, to put it slightly differently: would you take your car to a mechanic who could take your engine apart but couldn't put it back together again?

Textual Mechanics

Stalin called writers the "engineers of the soul". We might change the emphasis a little and say that Creative Writers and critical readers – and you can't be the first without being the second – are the mechanics of the text. They are interested in questions like: how does this thing work? If that bit goes here, how can it be connected to this bit? That is to say: in Creative Writing we both take the engine apart and put it back together again. The point is not necessarily to make a car that somebody might want to buy – although it is very gratifying when this happens – but to understand better how the car works. This kind of practical, hands-on understanding inevitably leads to a heightened critical appreciation of the objects of literary study.

Wonder

Reading and writing literature is, of course, not only a question of "mechanics". Wallace Stevens once said that he wished people would respond to poems the way that children respond to snow when they see it for the first time. Creative Writing can help to produce and sustain this sense of wonder, which is surely central to any experience and appreciation of works of verbal art. The sonnets of WYATT and SHAKESPEARE or WORDSWORTH and KEATS are all the more extraordinary to those who have tried to write sonnets themselves, just as the narrative craft and precision of KATHERINE MANSFIELD and FLANNERY O'CONNOR is especially manifest to someone who is writing or has written a short story. The practice of Creative Writing produces discriminating and demanding readers, but also readers who will pause to wonder at the very nuts and bolts of literary accomplishment. Without this sense of wonder, we could apply all our critical skills and methodologies to bus tickets and jam-jar labels and it wouldn't make any difference.

At the same time as encouraging this sense of wonder, the practice of Creative Writing also offers a very useful and effective challenge to much of the mythology of the creative artist as "genius". One still hears in literary critical seminars the objection: but did the writer really think about all this? This is usually an objection to what is perceived to be over-interpretation – writers aren't really conscious of all these things, it's more just inspiration…. As soon as you sit down to write yourself, however, you realize that there are highly conscious decisions to be taken at every stage. This is especially true once you come to rewrite what you have written, or when you work in a group whose members are forever asking you why you did this or that to your character or imagery or rhyme-scheme. And the idea of the workshop isn't new. Writer's have always got together to discuss their work, just think of the Lake Poets, or GOETHE and SCHILLER working on ballads, or BYRON and MARY and PERCY-BYSSHE SHELLEY writing supernatural tales by Lake Geneva, or EZRA POUND getting T. S. ELIOT to rewrite *The Waste Land.*

Genius

Creative Writing practices can offer a very direct complement to critical reading, and can be very effectively incorporated into literary critical seminars. A very simple bread-and-butter exercise such as rewriting a scene in a story from different character perspectives can provide a very direct and economical way of understanding the concept of perspective or "focalization" in narrative fiction. One might use several of the rewriting exercises developed in Chapter 4 in a similar fashion. One of the very best ways of understanding the ins and outs of a given literary style is to attempt to parody it, and then compare the parody with the original. A good way of understanding how a story begins or ends is to rewrite the beginning or the ending and look at how the whole story is affected. Similarly, a useful way into the historical and social setting of a poem is to re-set the poem in time – to write a 21st century version of an Elizabethan sonnet, for example, as we did in Chapter 7. One can do the same thing with space. How does transplanting a poem or story into a different geographical or cultural context change the meaning of the original? What does it tell us about the importance of the original location?

Writing as Reading

Or, for a more extended example, try the following exercise on characterization:

In a narrative fiction seminar, each participant invents a character and writes a two-line, explicit third-person characterization beginning with the words "S/he is the kind of person who…." This characterization is then passed to the next participant on the left. The second participant (who has already written a third-person characterization of their own and passed it on) now continues the

Exercise

characterization they have just been given, but this time in the first person. That is, they add to the characterization they have been given a further two lines beginning "I'm the kind of person who....". " This is now passed to the next person on the left, who adds to the character profile an *implicit* first-person self-characterization in which the character reveals something important about him/herself by describing another person, object or event. The character profile is then passed to the left again. This time the task is to write an implicit third-person characterization based on action; i.e., two or three lines in which the character *does* something which reveals a further aspect of his or her character. The profiles move on again and this time a piece of self-characterizing interior monologue is added. For example, the character is waiting for a bus, late for an appointment; what are the thoughts running through his or her head? With the next move, the task is to add a piece of second-person characterization in the form of an accusation. The character accuses someone of something and in doing so unwittingly tells us something more about him- or herself. The profile is handed on one more time, and the character is shown in dialogue with someone else, in which, again, further characteristics are revealed.

All the participants will now have before them a character profile with seven different pieces (and types) of characterization. If there are twenty people in the class, there will be twenty character profiles and 140 individual pieces of characterization. The whole process will have taken between half an hour and 40 minutes. The seminar will not only have provided a practical introduction to some of the central possibilities of characterization in fiction, but also have produced a fund of individual characterizations that can be collected, made available to all, and then sifted through and drawn upon in the writing of short stories.

The Stuff of Language

Finally, on the subject of Creative Writing and the study of literary texts, the writing of imaginative literature fosters a heightened awareness of the medium one is dealing with – of the materiality of language. In writing literary essays one's aim is to transmit information as directly and economically as possible. In Creative Writing, the communication of information as such is only one aspect of the process. One is also working with shape and pattern and form, with sound and rhythm and cadence. One learns very quickly that literary artefacts are not merely messages to be decoded, but often actually stand or fall by facets that lie beyond interpretation. When one has squeezed all the meaning apparently possible out of a poem or short story, one has not, by any means, got to the end of the matter. What makes a piece of Creative Writing memorable is, as often as not, not what it says, but how it says it. As ARCHIBALD MACLEISH wrote in his well-known "Ars

Poetica" (1926): "A poem should not mean / But be." It is precisely this heightened sense of the *being* of literary language that the practice of Creative Writing can very usefully cultivate.

Creative Writing and Literary Theory

We spoke earlier of how Creative Writing is not just about taking texts apart, but also about putting them back together again. To a degree, of course, this is true of any act of reading. Literary texts do not come to us as ready-made, fixed entities that simply demand decoding. All readings are also constructions of the text, and the reading process is in itself fundamentally creative. In this way, Creative Writing is a bit like reading in slow motion. It is, furthermore, a way of putting together our broader reading of texts in general, and of the world and our experience of it, most of which is already transmitted to us or processed in a basically textual form – even if only through the words we always already have for most of the things we experience. This eminently reasonable reflection has led, in some literary theoretical circles, to some pretty drastic conclusions about the nature of authorship.

Reading in Slow Motion

For a time at least, it became almost a commonplace in post-structuralist literary theory and criticism to speak of "the death of the author". The phrase derives from an essay of that title by ROLAND BARTHES from 1968, but the notion that the author is not the ultimate or most important originator of the literary text became extremely widespread, especially after the publication of MICHEL FOUCAULT's "What is an Author?" in 1969.

The Death of the Author

What is one to make of such a notion when facing a seminar full of ostensibly living and vehemently present authorial egos? The answer begins to emerge as soon as these authors start writing. As soon as they begin to express themselves in writing, it is almost inevitably someone else's self that comes out: a self full of preconceptions, full of other people's ideas and voices. This is not merely because our authors are no good at what they're doing. Many of the very best writers have experienced the same problem. When, at the beginning of his career, SAMUEL BECKETT put pen to paper, what came out was JAMES JOYCE. That was one of the reasons why BECKETT started writing in French.

The act of writing, when performed critically in the Creative Writing environment, forces us to recognize very quickly that we are not ourselves in quite the way we thought we were. We realize that our "we" or "I" – that most personal of pronouns – is not as free, independent and individual as we thought. Being a subject involves both being an agent, a doer, a maker, and being subjected to someone or something else – the voices of others, the weight of

The Subject in Question

the past, the pressures and limits of language itself. This is not, of course, new knowledge. It is implicit in the very word "subject", from Latin *sub* (under, beneath) and *jacere* (to throw).

Throwing Voices

The Creative Writing seminar is an excellent forum in which to explore this fundamental duality of the subject (that which is at once agent and instrument, origin and effect). Creative Writing is all about finding a voice. And just as when we begin to express ourselves, someone else's self jumps out, so when we try to find our voices, the voice that comes first is never truly our own. We cannot speak without quoting others. Every word we use is, to quote the Russian theorist MIKHAIL BAKHTIN, "overpopulated" with the inflections and intentions of millions of other users, past and present. We are like ventriloquists, throwing our voices, implicitly mimicking others whenever we speak.

It is not surprising that our voices are always thrown voices. We are, as the philosopher MARTIN HEIDEGGER reminds us, "thrown" into the world of language in the first place. We did not choose the world of relations and codes and norms in which we find ourselves. The act of writing is a perpetual reminder of how little of our own – and how much of being thrown – there is in what we say.

Creative Writing and Ventriloquism

One of the very first tasks of a Creative Writing workshop is to get the participants to hear the extent to which they write in thrown – borrowed, adopted, appropriated – voices. This happens regularly enough when we say to each other: "isn't that something of a cliche?" or "that doesn't really sound like you," or "that sounds a bit too much like NICK HORNBY." But we also try to hear the traces of others in our speech by quite deliberately throwing our voices. That is to say, we take the thrownness of voice on board and experiment with conscious acts of textual ventriloquism, such as stylistic imitation, caricature or parody. This kind of ventriloquism is, of course, part and parcel of the writer's never-ending endeavour to imagine him or herself into the shoes of another.

Exercise

Here is a very radical exercise for reinventing oneself in the voice of another, which I learnt from a workshop given by the writer MICHÈLE ROBERTS. Each participant has to write down the name of the most heinous form of crime that they can think of. It should be a crime they feel strongly about and object to at a deeply personal level. Once they have written down the name of the crime, the participants are asked to write a short piece – no more than a page – in the first person, in the persona of a criminal who has just committed or is about to commit the crime in question. This is stretching the idea of imagining oneself into another just about as far as it will go.

In practising ventriloquistic exercises of this kind, we are aiming above all at two things. First, to move as freely and imaginatively as possible across a range of thrown voices, and secondly to begin to hear the "own" in "thrown". The more we write out of ourselves, the more we realize that there are certain concerns, images and inflections that none the less keep on persisting, even when we are consciously striving against those voices we know to have influenced us. While there is no such thing as one's own pure and unadulterated voice, there will always be those particular constellations of echoes and inflections which respond most fully to the particularities of what we have to say and the means we have at our disposal to say it. This is the voice we are looking for, whose range we are seeking to sound. In other words we are striving for what HÖLDERLIN called "der freie Gebrauch des Eigenen", while recognizing, with HÖLDERLIN, that this is the hardest thing of all to achieve.

The Own in Thrown

③ Creative Writing and the New English Studies

The range of "writings" that constitutes the object of English Studies has probably never been as broad as it is today. The idea that only the great canonical literary works of the past are worthy of critical study has been vigorously challenged and the textual corpus has grown to include genres from hip-hop to hyptertext, from cyberpunk to cinema.

The Object of Study

In this context it is surely remarkable that the types of writing practised in the university have remained so limited. To the plethora of new writings that go together to make up the new collective object of study, we continue to respond with the critical or scholarly essay, with a critical structure and theoretical language primarily developed to explore a very different species of textual object. I am not suggesting that if you are writing about rap lyrics you should write in the *argot* of an MTV presenter, or if you are writing about Scottish Detective Fiction you should address the reader as Jimmy, Pal, or Hen. What I would suggest, however, is that the critical rigour we have applied to the deconstruction of the traditional canon needs to be applied to our own writing activity in the university. To criticize the white, male, bourgeois Western literary canon as exclusive and elitist is all very well; but we should not imagine the traditional discourses of literary scholarship to be any more inclusive (or any less elitist).

The Range of Response

| **A Plurality of Writings** | The critical essay is, without doubt, an absolutely essential form of critical exploration and response in the university study of literature. It is also in itself a highly valuable discipline of thought. But it still doesn't have to be the only form of writing with which we respond to other texts. Just as we have been working towards increased plurality in the spectrum of writings that constitute the object of our discipline, so we need to open up the writings of critical response. Here, Creative Writing, and creative thinking, have an important role to play. A critical dialogue, a stylistic imitation, a piece of directed rewriting, to give just three examples, could all form valuable parts of a more pluralistic and open-minded critical engagement with the texts and contexts being studied. |

| *Envoi* | All writing is a dialogue with other writing as well as with the world we live in. It is an enriching dialogue that helps us better to understand the past that has shaped us and the present that is partly ours to shape. Participation in this dialogue is the ultimate justification for Creative Writing, whether as a university discipline, a life-time vocation, or a clandestine obsession. Practiced with integrity, Creative Writing teaches us to listen more closely, to be constructively critical, to appreciate the "drunkenness of things being various", and to take delight in being surprised by others and ourselves. HENRY JAMES'S closing words of advice to the young writer in "The Art of Fiction" are as pertinent today as they were 120 years ago: *Be generous and delicate and pursue the prize.* (JAMES 1963: 97) |

Appendix: Creative Writing Workshops

As we said in the last chapter, writers have always come together to share and discuss their work. The formalized institution of the university Creative Writing workshop may be a twentieth century phenomenon, but the writer's need for dialogue with fellow practitioners is as old as the art of writing itself. In this section, I should like to say a few words about the function and value of Creative Writing workshops, and give one example of an extended workshop idea.

Introduction

1 The Focus of Workshops

It is essential that a Creative Writing workshop should be fully aware of what it is trying to achieve. Workshops vary enormously in purpose. Some aim primarily to steer writers towards publication, while others simply offer a forum for a group of friends to express their feelings and tell their own personal stories.

Purpose

Inevitably a Creative Writing workshop within a university undergraduate English Studies course will share rather different aims. JON COOK, one of the most eloquent champions of Creative Writing as a form of literary critical exploration offers this succint summary of the central aims of a university writing workshop:

To complement critical enquiry with some creative experiment, to understand a literary form in terms of craft and technique, both compositional act and cultural process. (BELL and MAGRS 2001: 300)

In pursuing these aims, I have found it useful in workshops to concentrate on the following three areas: practical writing exercises, discussion of work-in-progress and critical analysis of contemporary published texts.

Practical Writing

Whatever the focus of a Creative Writing workshop within a given semester, I like to make sure that some impromptu writing is done in every session. Timed writing exercises are extremely valuable for the following reasons.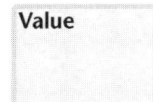

Value

Above all, they take the pressure off writers to meet their own (often unreal) expectations of producing polished pieces of work. It is essential that everyone involved understands that the purpose of timed exercises is not to write a masterpiece. Once participants accept that they not only cannot, but are not meant to, write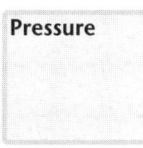

Pressure

something stunningly brilliant in twenty minutes, they are much freer in what they do.

Imagination

The constraints of time and theme involved in in-session writing experiments are also great liberators of the imagination. It is a paradox proved by nearly all workshop exercises that the tighter the hands of the participants are tied, the more freely their imagination tends to work. Ask a group to build a sonnet around fourteen given rhyming words and you can be sure that they will come up with ideas they would never have dreamed of on their own. Get them to write a 100-word autobiography using only monosyllabic words and the simple present tense and they will be forced to represent their lives in a radically new light.

Preconceptions

Workshop exercises also force writers to challenge and write beyond their own preconceptions. Experiments in impersonation can be very valuable here. Writing as a serial killer, as a member of the opposite sex, as a child, as a man with a broken leg trying to get on a bus – can all encourage writers to see the world from a different angle. It is equally beneficial to get writers who are preoccupied with big issues or feelings to write about simple objects, to describe in detail a stain on the carpet, or a desk, or a shoe. This is also a good way of getting writers to understand that issues and feelings can often be more convincingly expressed when they are anchored in concrete things rather than abstract ideas.

Surprise

Working under time pressure with rigid constraints of theme and form nearly always generates surprises. Not only do writers say things they'd otherwise never thought of saying, but they also discover interests they didn't know they had. The recognition that you have a great deal to say about your first bed, or about the way the feel of a leaf on your lips reminds you of kissing your granny good night can be revelatory. A writing exercise chosen by someone else can open up a constellation of interests you would never have entertained sitting alone at your desk.

Expectations

It is clearly crucial, for all the reasons given above, not to expect too much from in-session exercises. But nor should one expect too little. It needs to be made clear from the start that these exercises have one very important purpose beyond merely removing pressure and freeing the imagination. In whatever piece of guided writing you do in a workshop – from automatic writing, to experiments with strict form – the hope is always that there will be one phrase, one metaphor, one rhythm, one echo, that you will be able to make use of in your own work – one spark that goes on firing your imagination when you get it home to your desk.

Work-in-Progress

I also reserve one part of nearly every Creative Writing workshop for the discussion of work-in-progress. The work-in-progress is generally work assigned from the previous workshop session and completed by the participants in their own time. Usually the assignments are directly related to the overall focus of the workshop series.

The point of in-session discussions of work-in-progress is to provide the writer with constructive criticism of his or her work. One of the essential functions of any Creative Writing workshop is to train writers both to give and take constructive criticism. For criticism to be constructive, it needs to recognize what the piece of writing under discussion is seeking to do. Criticism is most helpful and effective when it is local and particular and in line with the overall aspirations of the piece of work in question. It is less helpful to say of a short story: "I don't like the character Jill", than to say: "from what the story tells us about Jill, it seems unlikely that she would use a word like *rapacious*."

We all tend to be attached to the things we have written, especially when they are still hot from the pen. Listening and responding constructively to criticism involves a certain amount of letting go. There are various ways of cultivating a more disinterested attitude to our own work in a Creative Writing workshop. One is to begin by discussing writing that has been produced collaboratively, such as the results of the haiku-to-sonnet exercise described in Chapter 7. Another way is to divide the workshop up into "angels" and "devils". Regardless of what they think of the piece under discussion, angels have to say something positive, while devils have to find fault. Here, adverse criticism is softened by being seen as a function of an exercise, rather than an expression of malice.

Reading Published Texts

In addition to the discussion of work-in-progress, I find it very important to discuss published writing in Creative Writing workshops. It is absolutely essential that beginning writers should be familiar with the published work of their contemporaries. This is particularly true of poetry workshops. It is more or less impossible to write poetry that can be read with pleasure by our peers without having a broad knowledge of the contemporary poetry scene. Much of the most forgettable poetry produced in Creative Writing workshops is simply oblivious of where poetry has been going over the last fifty years and deaf to the idiom of our age.

Critical Practice	As the appreciation of contemporary literature is so important, it is often inevitable that some workshop sessions will resemble seminars in practical criticism. This is especially true when dealing with groups who are not well trained in close reading. However, the emphasis in reading-based workshops needs to be directed as quickly as possible towards practical issues of writing. That is to say, the group must be encouraged to read as practitioners, rather than armchair critics. This is, of course, only possible once the basics of critical appreciation have already been grasped.

② Some Ground Rules for Workshops

Caution	The nature of a workshop will always be determined by the character and aims of its participants. The suggestions made in this section are not intended prescriptively. They constitute merely some basic "rules of thumb" which I believe to be productive rather than restrictive to any workshop practice.
"Do's and Don'ts"	In *The Creative Writing Handbook* (SINGLETON and LOCKHURST 1996), the poet and teacher LIZ ALMOND offers six very sensible workshop "ground rules" that are worth quoting in full:

1. *Observe silence when writing in a workshop – creative thought is disturbed by superficial conversation.*

2. *Always try to write as much as possible in the given time – the movement of pen on page sometimes produces material you had no idea was there. You are not just working with the conscious mind.*

3. *Don't be too self-conscious about the work produced – it's raw, waiting to be worked on, you're not trying to prove anything.*

4. *Be supportive of each other, be constructively critical, not negative.*

5. *Do not use the workshop as an opportunity to show off technical virtuosity – it intimidates other people.*

6. *Do not refuse to read your work out week after week or it will become an increasingly frightening prospect.* (SINGLETON and LOCKHURST 1996: 21–22)

Two Additions	To this list I would add two further observations. First, don't judge the group too quickly. It takes a few weeks for a group to settle and for its true character and potential to emerge. Secondly, take notes during workshops, particularly – but not only – when your own work is being discussed. It is crucial to take a second look at the comments of others on your work; give yourself the opportunity to come back to them, after the heat of the moment, with a clear head at home. Just as importantly, however, jot down anything

of interest you hear in a workshop, from a striking word association in someone else's exercise, to a particularly helpful way of formulating criticism. Be prepared to go up to other participants and ask them if they mind you developing one of their ideas.

3 Sample Workshop

I should like to close with a brief description of a workshop idea that I have used several times at the University of Cologne. It is offered as an example of how Creative Writing workshops can be planned as full semester courses within the university English Studies framework.

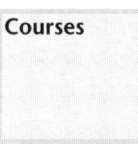
Courses

The Collective Town

In this workshop, the participants spend the whole semester working on short stories set in the same collectively imagined town. The aim is to produce a volume of interrelated stories, drawing upon a pool of collectively decided characters, locations and events.

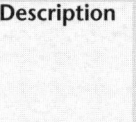
Description

In the first few weeks of the course, part of each workshop is devoted to the process of gathering ideas about the topography, history and inhabitants of the town. In the first session, we decide on a location and name for the town, and we draw a rough map. For the next session, participants are asked to submit five key historical events that have gone into the shaping of the town. These are discussed in the second session, in which we make a selection of the most promising ideas and draw up a table of historical events. For the third session, participants submit character portfolios. From these we select the most interesting characters as the inhabitants of the town who will figure in our stories.

Preliminaries

The participants then set about writing their interrelated stories. Part of each workshop is reserved for progress reports that will allow different writers to coordinate related material. Thus each writer's emerging narrative will have the chance to influence and be influenced by the work of others. Much of the discussion can be done in smaller groups of writers working with similar constellations of characters or events.

The Writing Process

The rest of the session is devoted to basic exercises in short story writing – exercises on topics like characterization, setting, perspective, style, beginnings and endings as described Chapter 3.

Participants are asked to write two stories. The first is submitted half way through the semester and discussed by the whole group.

Each participant then writes a second story inspired by the first story of another participant. The second story should either be a sequel or historical prequel to the chosen first story.

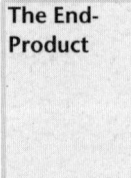

The End-Product

The aim is to end up with an intertextual anthology of stories in very different styles, but based on a number of shared locations, recurring events and reappearing characters. The stories should be coordinated enough to prevent one character from getting married at forty-five in one story and dying of rat poison at twenty-two in another. They should, however, also be sufficiently independent to leave room for unexpected turns of character and event.

Bibliography

Anthologies of Poetry and Prose

BRADBURY, Malcolm (ed): *The Penguin Book of Modern Short Stories*. Harmondsworth: Penguin 1988

FERGUSON, Margaret, SALTER, Mary Jo, and STALLWORTHY, Jon (eds): *The Norton Anthology of Poetry*. New York: W.W. Norton (Fourth Edition) 1996

HULSE, Michael, KENNEDY, David, and MORLEY, David (eds): *The New Poetry*. Newcastle upon Tyne: Bloodaxe 1993

KEEGAN, Paul (ed): *The New Penguin Book of English Verse*. Harmondsworth: Penguin 2002

MORRISON, Blake, and MOTION, Andrew (eds): *The Penguin Book of Contemporary British Poetry*. Harmondsworth: Penguin 1982

VENDLER, Helen (ed): *The Faber Book of Contemporary Poetry*. London: Faber and Faber 1990

Secondary Literature

ALLEN, Walter (ed): *Writers on Writing*. London: J.M. Dent 1948

AUDEN, W.H: *The Dyer's Hand*. New York: Random House 1962.

BALDWIN, Michael: *The Way to Write Stories*. London: Hamish Hamilton 1987

BELL, Julia, and MAGRS, Paul (eds): *The Creative Writing Coursebook*. London: Macmillan 2001

BOYLEN, Clare (ed): *The Agony and the Ego: The Art and Strategy of Fiction Writing Explored*. Harmondsworth: Penguin 1993

BRANDE, Dorothea: *Becoming a Writer*. London: Macmillan 1996

HARTLEY WILLIAMS, John, and SWEENEY, Matthew: *Writing Poetry and Getting Published*. London: Teach Yourself Books, Hodder Headline 1997

HOLLANDER, John: *Rhyme's Reason: A Guide to English Verse*. New Haven: Yale University Press (Third Edition) 2000

JAMES, Henry: *Selected Literary Criticism*. (ed. Morris Shapira) Harmondsworth: Penguin 1963

NEWMAN, Jenny, CUSICK, Edmund, and LA TOURETTE, Aileen (Eds): *The Writer's Workbook*. London: Edward Arnold: London 2000

O'CONNOR, Flannery: *Mystery and Manners: Occasional Prose*. London: Faber and Faber 1972

POUND, Ezra: *ABC of Reading*. New York: New Directions Publishing 1968

SANSOM, Peter: *Writing Poems*. Newcastle upon Tyne: Bloodaxe (Third Impression) 1994

SINGLETON, John and LUCKHURST, Mary (eds): *The Creative Writing Handbook: Techniques for New Writers*. (Second Edition) Basingstoke: Palgrave 2000

SINGLETON, John: *The Creative Writing Workbook*. Basingstoke: Palgrave 2001